# Building Small Cabinets

DOUG STOWE

# Building Small Cabinets

The Taunton Press

The Taunton Press, Inc., 63 South Main Street, PO Box 5506, Newtown, CT 06470-5506

e-mail: tp@taunton.com

Editors: Helen Albert and Carolyn Mandarano
Copy editor: Candace B. Levy
Indexer: Jim Curtis
Jacket/Cover design: Kimberly Adis
Interior design: Kimberly Adis
Layout: Helen Albert
Illustrator: Melanie Powell
Photographer: Doug Stowe

Library of Congress Cataloging-in-Publication Data

Stowe, Doug.
  Building small cabinets / Doug Stowe.
    p. cm.
  ISBN 978-1-60085-347-0 (pbk.)
 1.  Cabinetwork.  I. Title.
 TT197.S86 2011
 684.1'6--dc23

                        2011031058

Printed in the United States of America
10 9 8 7 6 5 4 3 2 1

The following manufacturers/names appearing in *Building Small Cabinets* are trademarks:
Ace Hardware®, Amerock®, Brusso®, Elmer's®, Glue-All®, Rockler™, Stanley®, Woodcraft®.

Working with wood is inherently dangerous. Using hand or power tools improperly or ignoring safety practices can lead to permanent injury or even death. Don't try to perform operations you learn about here (or elsewhere) unless you're certain they are safe for you. If something about an operation doesn't feel right, don't do it. Look for another way. We want you to enjoy the craft, so please keep safety foremost in your mind whenever you're in the shop.

To all those who share my love of wood.

## ACKNOWLEDGMENTS

**I WISH TO EXTEND MY VERY SPECIAL THANKS TO MY EDITOR,**
Helen Albert. I have had the pleasure of working with her on four books.
How-to books require a team effort, and I've been working with the very
best. I'm very grateful for the support of the editorial and production team
at Taunton Press, especially Carolyn Mandarano, Katy Binder, and Sharon
Zagata. Special thanks also to David Heim, friend and former editor at *Fine
Woodworking*, who helped to refine my illustrations and do some of the
things with the drawing software that left Helen and me scratching our
heads. Many thanks to Melanie Powell, the illustrator, for rendering these
complex drawings.

# Contents

2   Introduction

4   **Shaker Pegboard Cabinet**
6   Mill the stock
7   Rabbet the top and bottom
8   Make the sides
9   Make and fit the hanger
14  Make the back panel
15  Sand and rout the edges
16  Assemble the sides
17  Hinge the door
20  Assemble and finish

22  **Key House**
25  Build the cabinet box
31  Build the doors

34  **Panel-Door Spice Cabinet**
36  Cut the biscuit joints
37  Fit the back
38  Make the shelves
40  Shape the top and bottom
42  Assemble the carcase
42  Make the door components
47  Shape and assemble the doors
49  Make and install the hanger
49  Rout the hinge mortises
51  Install the stop
52  Finish

54  **Cherry Display Cabinet**
57  Make the top and bottom
60  Make the sides and door post
61  Build the doors
66  Make the shelves and liners
69  Prepare for assembly
70  Assemble the cabinet
71  Complete the doors

## 74 Mission Display Cabinet

77    Make the sides

79    Make the top and bottom

81    Make the doors and front panel

85    Shape the top and bottom

86    Prepare for assembly

88    Assemble and finish

90    A contemporary variation

## 92 Greene and Greene Cabinet

95    Build a finger-joint jig

97    Build the sides and top

100    Build the doors

104    Assemble the carcase

106    Hinge and trim the doors

107    Pin the doors

108    Install the tie hanger

109    A tool-cabinet alternative

## 111 Jelly Cabinet

115    Build the frames

117    Make the carcase panels

119    Complete the carcase assemblies

123    Make the top, bottom, and shelf

124    Assemble the carcase

125    Make the moldings

128    Assemble and install the top

129    Build the doors

133    Prepare for the hardware and shelves

## 134 Krenov-Inspired Cabinet

137    Cut the dovetail joints

140    Complete the carcase

144    Build the base

147    Build the doors

152    Make the drawer

153    Final details

## 154 Metric Equivalents

# INTRODUCTION

**BIGGER THAN A BREADBOX,** small cabinets are perfect to fine-tune skills and explore woodworking techniques. They can be as easy as a simple box or as complex as the very finest things made of wood.

My own relationship with making small cabinets began when I worked at a very small company making cabinets from recycled barn boards. I gradually developed some skill and design ideas of my own, and I began making small display cabinets for small shops and galleries. Most of those small cabinets are still in use today, either in the shops for which they were made or in our local historic museum.

One of the first things I made for my wife, a librarian, was a spice cabinet that allowed for spices to be put in alphabetical order in our kitchen. It is as beautiful today as the day it was made, so I can assure you that the small cabinets you make will become the family heirlooms that record your growth as a craftsman.

If you are a beginning woodworker, you will benefit from starting at the beginning of the book. As the chapters progress the projects are more difficult and more complex and thus more suited to intermediate and advanced skill levels. Each cabinet in this book can be easily adapted to multiple uses. Some of the techniques used can be borrowed from one project to the next to fit your own style of work or the tools in your own shop. For instance, the spice cabinet also can be made with mortise-and-tenon joints, or kept simple through the use of biscuit joinery or dowels. By substituting glass doors in place of panels, a small spice cabinet can become the perfect home for a small collection of interesting things.

As you build the projects in this book. use the materials lists as a guide, but measure your own assemblies as you build them. You may cut parts a little differently, which over a whole project can add up to a lot of difference. For accuracy, actual measurements are always the best.

It is said that a teacher's job is complete when his students surpass him. I wish you every success in designing and building your own small cabinets.

# Shaker Pegboard Cabinet

**O**SCAR WILDE said, "All beautiful things are made by those who strive to make something useful." As proof, we have the enduring beauty of Shaker furniture and cabinetry. The simple usefulness of Shaker work, combined with caring craftsmanship, gives it lasting appeal. This cabinet, inspired by an early example of Shaker work, is made from white oak, a wood favored by Shaker craftsmen.

In this project, you'll learn to cut parts to accurate lengths using a cut-off sled. You'll also learn to cut hinge mortises by hand. Many woodworkers avoid using nails in finer work, but the practical and efficient Shakers didn't shy away from using nails where appropriate. In honor of the original cabinet that inspired this project, I used nails that replicate the cut nails used during the early days of Shaker furniture design. You can easily make this small cabinet in your choice of woods, and you can scale it up to make it more useful.

# Shaker pegboard cabinet

Like many examples of small Shaker cabinetry, this cabinet is designed to hang from Shaker pegs for temporary rather than permanent placement. There's an angled ledger at the back, which makes the cabinet easy to hang and easy to remove for cleaning or painting.

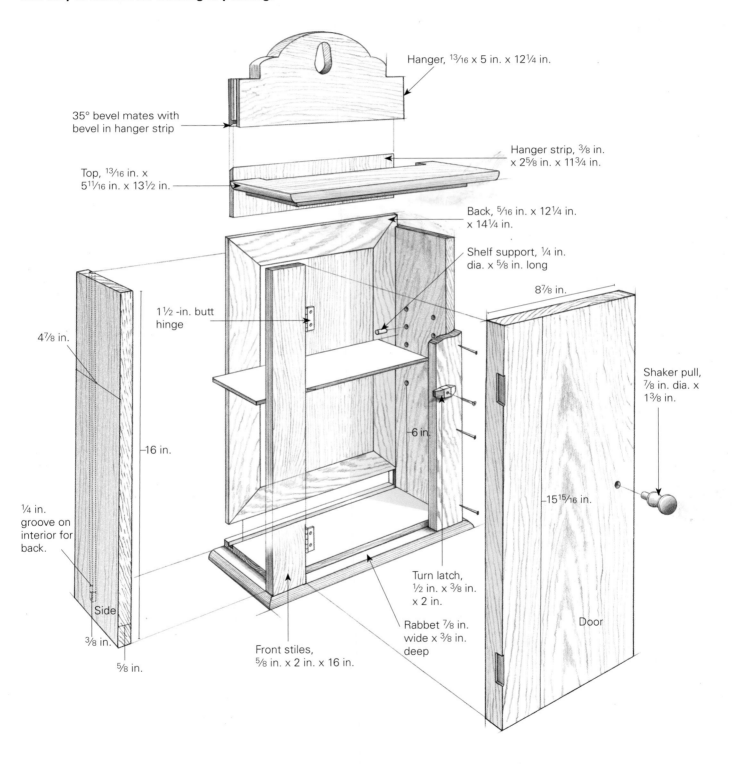

Hanger, $^{13}/_{16}$ x 5 in. x 12$^{1}/_{4}$ in.

35° bevel mates with bevel in hanger strip

Top, $^{13}/_{16}$ in. x 5$^{11}/_{16}$ in. x 13$^{1}/_{2}$ in.

Hanger strip, $^{3}/_{8}$ in. x 2$^{5}/_{8}$ in. x 11$^{3}/_{4}$ in.

Back, $^{5}/_{16}$ in. x 12$^{1}/_{4}$ in. x 14$^{1}/_{4}$ in.

Shelf support, $^{1}/_{4}$ in. dia. x $^{5}/_{8}$ in. long

8$^{7}/_{8}$ in.

1$^{1}/_{2}$ -in. butt hinge

4$^{7}/_{8}$ in.

Shaker pull, $^{7}/_{8}$ in. dia. x 1$^{3}/_{8}$ in.

16 in.

6 in.

$^{1}/_{4}$ in. groove on interior for back.

15$^{15}/_{16}$ in.

Side

$^{3}/_{8}$ in.

$^{5}/_{8}$ in.

Front stiles, $^{5}/_{8}$ in. x 2 in. x 16 in.

Turn latch, $^{1}/_{2}$ in. x $^{3}/_{8}$ in. x 2 in.

Rabbet $^{7}/_{8}$ in. wide x $^{3}/_{8}$ in. deep

Door

## MATERIALS FOR SHAKER PEGBOARD CABINET

| QUANTITY | PART | SIZE | NOTES |
|---|---|---|---|
| 2 | Front stiles | $\frac{5}{8}$ in. x 2 in. x 16 in. | White oak |
| 2 | Sides | $\frac{5}{8}$ in. x $4\frac{7}{8}$ in. x 16 in. | White oak |
| 2 | Top and Bottom | $\frac{13}{16}$ in. x $5\frac{11}{16}$ in. x $13\frac{1}{2}$ in. | White oak |
| 1 | Hanger | $\frac{13}{16}$ in. x 5 in. x $12\frac{1}{4}$ in. | White oak |
| 1 | Hanger strip | $\frac{3}{8}$ in. x $2\frac{5}{8}$ in. x $11\frac{3}{4}$ in. | White oak |
| 1 | Door | $\frac{9}{16}$ in. x $8\frac{7}{8}$ in. x $15\frac{15}{16}$ in. | White oak |
| 1 | Back | $\frac{15}{16}$ in. x $12\frac{1}{4}$ in. x $14\frac{1}{4}$ in. | White oak |
| 1 | Shelf | $\frac{3}{8}$ in. x $4\frac{1}{4}$ in. x $11\frac{3}{4}$ in. | White oak |
| 4 | Shelf supports | $\frac{1}{4}$ in. dia. x $\frac{5}{8}$ in. | Cut from wooden dowel |
| 1 | Shaker pull | $\frac{7}{8}$ in. dia. x $1\frac{3}{8}$ in. long | White oak |
| 1 | Turn latch | $\frac{1}{2}$ in. x $\frac{3}{8}$ in. x 2 in. | White oak |
| 2 | Brass hinges | $\frac{7}{8}$ in. x $1\frac{1}{2}$ in. | Ace Hardware® # 5299755 |
| 11 | Brass screws | #5 x 1 in. | |
| 18 | Cut nails | $1\frac{1}{2}$ in. long | |

# Mill the stock

**PREPARE YOUR STOCK FROM ROUGH-SAWN** lumber. If your wood is warped or twisted, pass it across the jointer first to make sure it is flat.

**A**

**PLANE THE STOCK TO THICKNESS. If it is warped, cut the parts slightly oversize in width and length, flatten on the jointer, and then plane.**

**1.** Plane your material to thickness from rough-sawn stock **(PHOTO A)**. Plane the top and bottom first. Then plane the sides after they have been sawn to width.

**2.** Use the jointer to flatten one edge to prepare for ripping your parts to size.

**3.** Rip parts to width on the tablesaw. For consistency, rip all parts of the same width, before resetting the rip fence.

**4.** Cut the parts to length using a cut-off sled and stop block to make sure the parts are exactly the required lengths.

# Rabbet the top and bottom

**MAKE THE FIRST CUTS** with the stock flat on the saw table. Begin with the short-grain sides. Then cut the long-grain side against the fence.

**RABBETS ON THREE SIDES OF THE TOP AND** bottom provide a strong connection with the sides and front and make the top and bottom appear thinner and lighter. The rabbets also create a positive stop for the door. The finished rabbet is ⅞ in. wide × ⅜ in. deep.

**1.** Set the height of the tablesaw blade to ⅜ in. and adjust the fence for a cut precisely ⅞ in. from the edge of the stock. Begin with the short-grain sides. Hold the end of the stock tightly to the fence while making the crosscuts with a miter gauge. Then make the long-grain cut on the front of each part **(PHOTO B)**.

**2.** Hold the parts on edge to finish the rabbet. Use a featherboard to keep the board tight to the fence. Raise the height of the tablesaw blade to ⅞ in. Set the rip fence ⁷⁄₁₆ in. from the blade. First cut the ends and then make the cut across the front **(PHOTO C)**.

**COMPLETE THE RABBETS** with the board on edge. Use a featherboard to steady the workpiece and hold it tight to the fence.

# Make the sides

**THE SHELF IN THIS CABINET IS ADJUSTABLE.**
Once the sides and front stiles have been dimensioned to length, you'll need to drill a series of holes to hold short dowels to support the shelf. You'll also cut grooves in the sides and bottom for the back.

**DRILL THE HOLES FOR DOWELS** to support adjustable shelves. Use the drill press and set the depth stop so the holes don't pass through the stock.

**1.** Carefully lay out the position of the holes on the sides and front pieces. The holes are set 1¾ in. from the back edge of the sides and ⅞ in. from the door-side edge of the front stiles. Lay out six holes, spaced 1 in. on center, with the bottom hole placed about 6 in. from the bottom of each piece. Once you've laid out one set of holes, use a square and pencil to transfer the markings from each piece to its mate.

## WORK SMART

When setting the depth of the drill press for drilling in thin stock, make sure to take into account the point of the bit, especially for a brad-point bit.

**2.** To drill the holes, use a drill press outfitted with a ¼-in.-dia. drill bit and a fence set to ensure a consistent distance from the edge of each piece. Drill the holes approximately ⅜ in. deep, making sure not to drill through the outside of the workpiece **(PHOTO A)**.

**3.** Cut the grooves for the back panel in the bottom and sides on the tablesaw. Set the rip fence ⅜ in. from the blade and adjust the blade to a ¼-in. depth. You could set up a dado blade to make the groove, but I simply make a cut and then widen it to ¼ in. with multiple adjacent cuts **(PHOTO B)**. This takes more time to cut the grooves, but saves the time needed to change blades. Note that you're cutting grooves only on the rear side of the bottom and the sides, not the top.

**USE THE TABLESAW TO CUT GROOVES** on the top, bottom, and sides for the back panel. Make one cut on each piece, then adjust the fence to make a second cut, widening the groove to ¼ in.

# Make and fit the hanger

**THE HANGER IS PARTIALLY CONCEALED** under the top and is connected to the sides with tenons. This design hides the joinery, while allowing for seasonal wood movement.

**1.** Begin by laying out the opening for the hanger at the rear of the top. The width will be determined by the shape you choose for the top of the hanger. I chose 1⅞ in. from the edge of the top. This dimension allows the visible part of the hanger to be 9¾ in. wide. The depth of the cut is equal to the thickness of the hanger: ¹³⁄₁₆ in.

**2.** Once you've established the position for the vertical cuts, set a stop block on the fence of the crosscut sled. This will ensure that the hanger opening is centered **(PHOTO A)**.

**3.** Draw a line from the top of one kerf to the other to define where you'll cut with the bandsaw to remove the waste. On the bandsaw, make an angled cut to the line, and then cut to the layout line, leav-

**A**

**USE A STOP BLOCK ON THE CROSSCUT SLED** to position the vertical cut. Cut one end and then the other. The stop block will ensure that the cuts are positioned equally from each end.

ing a bit of excess to be removed in a finishing cut. Then turn the stock and cut in from the other side **(PHOTO B)**.

**4.** To square up the opening, go back to the tablesaw and nibble away the waste in a series of passes. Take light overlapping cuts until you remove most of the waste. For a final cleanup, slide the stock over the blade as the saw is running and push the sled forward until the blade begins to cut **(PHOTO C)**. Then slide the workpiece away from the stop block until the cut is past the halfway point. Turn the piece end for end and repeat the process for the other side.

**B**

**USE A BANDSAW TO CUT AWAY THE WASTE** between the two tablesaw kerfs. Make an angled cut toward the line. Then cut to your layout line, staying well on the waste side of the line.

**C**

**SQUARE UP THE CUT.** I use the tablesaw outfitted with a flat-tooth-grind (FTG) blade. Make a series of passes. Take a light cut, slide the stock over, move the sled forward, and cut again.

# Cut the hanger joinery

**USE THE TABLESAW TO CUT THE TENON SHOULDERS** on the ends of the back hanger. Cut on one side, then flip the stock end to end to cut the other end. Adjust the height of the cut before making similar cuts on the opposite side.

**THE HANGER IS TENONED INTO THE SIDES** of the cabinet and fits into the same groove as the back. The tenons are offset so the hanger will be flush to the back edge of the sides. The tenon shoulders on the rear of the hanger are ³⁄₈ in. deep. On the front of the hanger, the shoulders are ³⁄₁₆ in. deep. Because the tenons are only ¼ in. long, you can cut them by gradually nibbling away the waste from the shoulder to the end of the tenon or you can use a tenoning jig (see p. 41 on how to build your own).

**1.** Set a stop block on the fence of a crosscut sled to limit the length of the tenon to ¼ in. Then set the blade height to ³⁄₈ in. to conform to the position of the groove cut in the cabinet sides. Flip the board end to end and cut the tenon shoulders on the opposite end. Then reset the height of the blade to ³⁄₁₆ in. to cut the tenon shoulders on the inside face of the hanger. **(PHOTO D).**

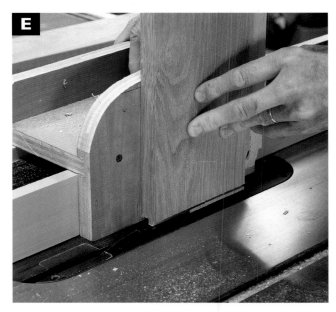

**USE A TENONING JIG TO CUT THE CHEEKS. First** cut one cheek then flip the workpiece end to end and cut the tenon on the opposite side. Reposition the fence to cut the tenon cheeks on the opposite face.

**CUT THE GROOVE** on the bottom of the hanger on the table-saw. Raise the blade to ½ in. deep. Widen the groove to the final ¼-in. dimension by moving the fence and making successive passes.

**2.** You can nibble away the waste from the tenon cheeks by making successive cuts with the face of the board on the crosscut jig, gradually moving the workpiece away from the blade with each pass. Or use a tablesaw tenoning jig on the tablesaw to cut the tenon cheeks **(PHOTO E)**.

**3.** Cut the ¼-in. groove for the back panel. Because the back of the hanger will be shaped to form a 35° bevel for hanging, cut this groove ½ in. deep (rather than ¼ in. deep like the grooves you cut in the cabinet sides and bottom). Again, widen the groove to ¼ in. by moving the fence to match the width of the groove cut in the cabinet sides and bottom **(PHOTO F)**.

**4.** A wooden auxiliary fence must be mounted to the rip fence to cut the 35° bevel on the bottom of the hanger and the top edge of the hanger strip. Adjust the angle of the blade to 35° and make a relief cut on the accessory fence, then clamp the fence in place, making certain the position of the clamps won't interfere with the movement of the workpiece through the cut. The workpiece is positioned with the back of the hanger on the table and the bottom facing the fence. Carefully align the saw cut to remove as little as possible while forming the 35° bevel **(PHOTO G)**. Without changing the set-

**MAKE A 35° CUT** across the back edge of the hanger. The back of the hanger is flat on the saw table.

ting of the saw, cut the 35° bevel at the top edge of the hanger strip. (For details on how these parts go together, see the drawing on p. 12.)

# Hanger detail

**Create a template to shape the top of the hanger. You can use these dimensions as a guide.**

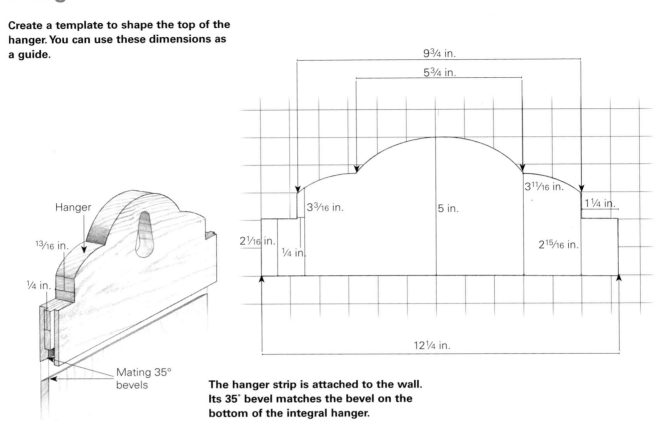

Hanger

13/16 in.

1/4 in.

Mating 35° bevels

9¾ in.

5¾ in.

3¹¹/16 in.

1¼ in.

3³/16 in.

5 in.

2¹/16 in.

¼ in.

2¹⁵/16 in.

12¼ in.

**The hanger strip is attached to the wall. Its 35° bevel matches the bevel on the bottom of the integral hanger.**

# Shaping the hanger

**1.** To begin shaping the hanger, you'll make a cut to define a ledge for the top to rest on in the assembled cabinet. To shape this ledge, measure 2¹/16 in. from the bottom edge of the hanger. You'll be making the cut with the hanger on end. Set a stop block on the fence of the crosscut box to ensure the distance is equal on both ends. Set the blade to cut to a depth of 1¼ in. (1 in. into the body of the hanger plus ¼ in. for the tenon) **(PHOTO H).** Draw a line, using a square, from the end of each saw kerf to the top of the hanger. This defines the shoulder of the ledge.

**MAKE CUTS INTO EACH END** to begin shaping the back hanger to fit the top of the cabinet.

CREATE A TEMPLATE FOR THE HANGER using folded paper and scissors. Then trace the shape onto the back hanger to prepare for sawing.

CUT THE BACK HANGER TO SHAPE on the band-saw. Stay on the waste side of the line to allow for final sanding and shaping.

**2.** Make a template for the shape of the top and trace it on the hanger **(PHOTO I)**.

**3.** Carefully cut the shape of the top on the band-saw **(PHOTO J)**.

**4.** Use a combination of belt and disk sanders to gradually taper the top of the hanger. Then drill holes through the center of the top with two drill

bits to form the key-hole shape for a Shaker peg **(PHOTO K)**.

**5.** Remove the waste between the two holes with a straight chisel **(PHOTO L)**. Work from one side, then from the other to avoid tearout.

**6.** Smooth the edge of the hanger with a sanding drum or rasp to remove any bandsaw marks.

DRILL TWO HOLES in the center of the hanger, one on top of the other, with the lower one being large enough to fit over the wide part of a shaker peg.

REMOVE THE WASTE between the holes with a straight chisel.

# Make the back panel

**THE BACK IS MADE OF RESAWN STOCK TO** conserve material. After gluing up the panel and planing it to final thickness, taper the edges so the back can fit into the grooves.

**USE A BANDSAW AND FENCE** to cut 4/4 stock down the middle to form book-matched panels.

**TIGHTEN THE CLAMPS** and check as you go that each board is level with its neighbors.

**1.** Saw rough 4/4 stock right down the middle, and you'll get boards about ⁹⁄₁₆ in. thick **(PHOTO A)**. Joint and plane the material until both sides are nearly smooth. Then joint the edges.

**2.** Prepare your clamps in advance of gluing. Spread a bead of glue on each board and clamp, checking that the boards remain flat and even as pressure is applied **(PHOTO B)**. Set the work aside while the glue dries (at least 45 minutes or longer). After the glue is fully dried, plane the back panel on both sides to a uniform thickness of ⁵⁄₁₆ in. and cut it to finished size.

**3.** Tilt the sawblade on the tablesaw to a 3° angle and make a bevel cut on four sides with the panel on edge **(PHOTO C)**. Adjust the cut until the edge will fit into the grooves cut into sides, bottom, and back hanger.

**CUT A 3° BEVEL ON THE PANEL** on the tablesaw. A high auxiliary fence, clamped to the regular rip fence, supports the workpiece and keeps your hands away from the blade.

# Sand and rout the edges

**SOFTENING THE EDGES OF THE TOP AND** bottom with a small-radius, roundover bit gives the cabinet a more finished look in keeping with Shaker traditional edge treatments.

**1.** Mount a ⅜-in.-dia. roundover bit in the router table to cut a profile on the edges of the top and bottom. The first pass will be made with the outside face (the top of the top and the bottom of the bottom) of the workpiece flat on the table. The second pass will be on the inside face with the workpiece on edge, between the fence and the bit **(PHOTO A)**. Take a light pass at first to make sure the roundover doesn't extend beyond where the front and sides meet these parts.

**A**

**USE A ROUNDOVER BIT IN THE ROUTER TABLE** to shape the edges of the top and bottom. First round the corners on the outside edges with the surfaces flat on the table. Then set the fence to rout the edges on the opposite face, passing the stock on edge between the fence and router bit.

**2.** Use a random-orbit sander to sand the edges of the hanger, bottom, and top to remove any tool marks and soften the corners **(PHOTO B)**, but avoid sanding too much, especially where the top will fit closely to other parts.

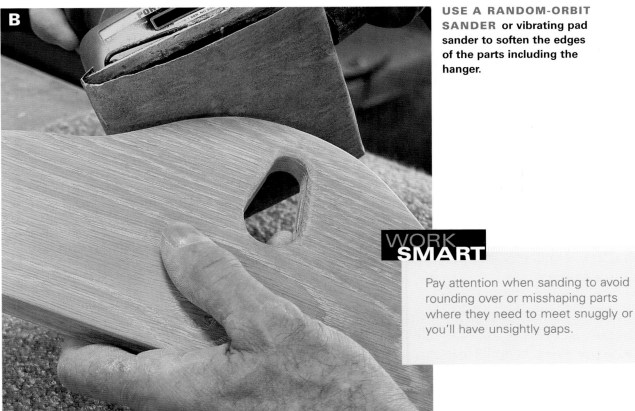

**B**

**USE A RANDOM-ORBIT SANDER** or vibrating pad sander to soften the edges of the parts including the hanger.

**WORK SMART**

Pay attention when sanding to avoid rounding over or misshaping parts where they need to meet snuggly or you'll have unsightly gaps.

# Assemble the sides

**BEFORE SANDING THE CABINET SIDES, GLUE** the front stiles to the sides, keeping them clamped until the glue sets. The edges must line up perfectly. Check and double-check as clamping pressure is applied to make sure the pieces haven't slipped.

**1.** Spread a bead of glue on the front of the side piece. (Make sure the groove is in the back.) Carefully align the front stile to the side piece. (Make sure the shelf pin holes are nearer the edge not being glued.) Clamp the two pieces together to the edge of your workbench. Check after clamping to make sure both parts are still in alignment **(PHOTO A)**. Allow the glue to fully set.

**2.** Drill ⅛-in.-dia. pilot holes in the front stiles for the square-cut nails to fit. These nails would split the wood if driven into fully dried hardwoods, so the accurately sized pilot holes are essential **(PHOTO B)**. Carefully, hammer in the nails.

**WHEN THE GLUE IS FULLY SET,** use a ⅛-in. drill bit to drill pilot holes for square-cut nails to be driven into place. In place of the nails, you could use ⅛-in. dowels, which would give the cabinet a different, but equally traditional look.

**GLUE THE FRONT** stiles to the sides. Be careful that the edges align during clamping and make any necessary adjustments as you apply pressure.

# Hinge the door

ALIGN THE POINT OF THE MARKING GAUGE to how much of the barrel you want to protrude. Then align it to define the depth to which the hinge will be recessed into the door.

MARK THE LENGTH of the mortise on the edge of the door. Use a square and pencil to make the marks.

DRAG THE POINT OF THE MARKING GAUGE between the pencil marks. This mark should be deep enough to provide a starting point for a chisel cut.

**INSTALLING ONE PAIR OF HINGES BY HAND** is just about as easy and quick as using other methods, especially when you figure in the time for machine setup. For a Shaker-inspired project like this, an occasion to show off your hand skills seems especially appropriate.

**1.** Transfer measurements from the hinge to the door, using a marking gauge. First, set the width of the mortise so that half the hinge barrel will protrude outside the cabinet. This protrusion allows the hinge to operate without binding **(PHOTO A)**.

**2.** Use a tape measure, square, and pencil to measure and mark the location of the hinge on the edge of the door. Make pencil tick marks where the hinge mortise is to start and stop. Then align the square to the pencil marks. Draw the lines and extend them onto the face of the stock so they can be used to transfer hinge markings to the cabinet sides as well **(PHOTO B)**.

**3.** Use the marking gauge to lay a gauge line between the lines **(PHOTO C)**.

The key to a clean gauge line is a sharp pin and good control. Angle the beam slightly and hold the fence tightly to the edge of the board.

**D**

**4.** Align the door in its actual position on the cabinet side so you can transfer the hinge locations from the pencil lines **(PHOTO D)**. When your hinge location is established, use the marking gauge to scribe the line at the back of the hinge mortise as you did on the door in the previous step.

**E**

**SET THE MARKING GAUGE** to just under half the thickness of the barrel of the hinge.

**MARK THE EDGE OF THE DOOR** and the edge of the cabinet side for the depth of the hinge mortise by pulling the mortising gauge between the pencil marks. The marking gauge will score a line, giving the chisel a positioning point where you'll begin the cut from the edge.

**5.** Adjust the marking gauge so that the pin is set to slightly less than half the thickness of the hinge barrel. You can do this by aligning the pin to the midpoint of the hinge pin and then back off a bit **(PHOTO E)**. Another simple technique uses a dial caliper to measure the overall thickness of the closed hinge at the barrel. Divide that measurement by half and subtract $\frac{1}{64}$ in. to $\frac{1}{32}$ in. for clearance. Then set the marking gauge to match this measurement. Remember that the actual amount of clearance doubles because you have two hinge mortises, one on the door and the other on the cabinet side.

**6.** Use that marking-gauge setting to scribe the depth of the mortise, moving between the pencil marks on the edge of the door and the edge of the cabinet side **(PHOTO F)**.

**F**

# Cut the hinge mortises

**1.** Use a straight chisel to cut at the pencil lines on both sides of the hinge mortise and then across the back. Then use the chisel to make a series of cuts down to the marking gauge line on the edge of the stock **(PHOTO G)**. Holding the chisel at an angle allows each cut to lift and loosen adjoining stock slightly to be more easily removed in the next step.

**2.** Use a wide chisel to pare in from the edge to complete the hinge mortise, using the gauge line as the guide for aligning the tip **(PHOTO H)**. Be careful to keep the other hand safely out of the way in the event that the chisel slips. If your relief cuts have been made to the full depth of the marking gauge line, the material in the mortise will lift out with little effort. Clean up any extra material, making sure the bottom of the mortise is flush to the gauge line. Repeat these steps for all four mortises.

G

H

**MAKE A SERIES OF CUTS** down to the marking gauge line along the edge. If the chisel is held at a slight angle as shown, it will lift pieces for easy removal in the next step.

**MAKE A PARING CUT** into the mortise from the edge using the gauge line as a reference point.

# Install the hinges

**1.** Use a self-centering drill bit to drill the pilot holes for the hinge screws. If you don't have a self-centering bit, mark the center of the hole using an awl and use a drill bit sized slightly smaller than the screws. Offset the point of the bit slightly toward the back of the hinge mortise so the screws will pull the hinge tightly into place **(PHOTO I)**.

**2.** Carefully drive the screws with a correctly sized hand-held screwdriver.

Brass screws are soft and easily damaged. Try coating them with some wax before driving them. You could also drive a steel screw of exactly the same size and then replace it with the brass screw.

I

**HOLD THE HINGE TIGHTLY** into the back of the mortise as you drill the holes so the hinge will be pulled tight when the screws go into place.

# Assemble and finish

**DRIVE THE SQUARE NAILS** into the shoulders of the rabbet in the top and bottom parts. Make sure all parts are in correct position before driving the nails.

**BEFORE ASSEMBLING THE CABINET, MAKE** certain that all of the inside surfaces are sanded and ready for finishing. You won't get a chance to sand inside after the parts are permanently attached. Once the sanding is done, assemble the cabinet around the back panel.

**A SIMPLE TURN KEY** made from scrap wood keeps the door closed. Make sure to orient the long grain as shown in the photo.

**1.** Arrange the parts and clamp them in position. Drill ⅛-in. pilot holes for the antique-style square nails. Drill these pilot holes to the full depth of the nails to prevent splitting the wood.

**2.** Drive the square nails carefully to avoid marring the wood surface **(PHOTO A)**.

**3.** Make a turn key out of scrap wood. Drill through the center for a brass screw. Taper the ends on the bandsaw and round the corners on a stationary belt sander or an inverted pad sander. The shape of the key isn't critical. This sort of key is found on many country pieces and it is a simple but effective means of keeping the door closed **(PHOTO B)**.

**4.** Turn a Shaker knob on the lathe using matching white oak. This is a simple and fun exercise that will improve your turning skills. The only hard part is sizing the tenon to fit a hole in the door of the cabinet. Use an open-end wrench as a gauge to help size the tenon to fit **(PHOTO C)**. Don't be discouraged if you shape the tenon too small. Try again with a smaller wrench and choose the appropriately sized drill bit when you are ready to install the knob. If you don't have a lathe, look for factory-made Shaker knobs like the one shown in the cherry variation at right, or choose a porcelain or glass pull from your woodworking supplier or hardware store.

**5.** Apply the finish of your choice. A penetrating oil finish seems especially appropriate for Shaker-style work.

**6.** To hang the cabinet, screw the hanger strip to the wall with flat-head screws, with at least one screw into the wall stud. Make sure the wider part of the cleat faces out and the hanger strip is level on the wall. Slip the back edge of the integral hanger until it engages the cleat.

**USE AN OPEN-END WRENCH** as a guide to size the knob tenon to a standard drill bit.

## A CHERRY VARIATION

The Shaker wall cabinet can be made in a variety of sizes, but larger ones may not lend themselves to the use of Shaker pegs for hanging due to weight and size. For this cherry cabinet, I chose to ignore the holes at the top, making the back hanger with very simple ornamentation in keeping with the simplicity of Shaker design.

A center divider allows you to add a second door, increasing the width of the cabinet and its usefulness. In place of antique nails, I chose to use ³⁄₁₆-in. dowels to secure the parts. Instead of a solid wood back, I used Baltic-birch plywood.

**THIS VARIATION** features dowel pins instead of cut nails, double doors, and stock Shaker knobs from a woodworking supplier. Notice how the turn key can secure both doors.

# Key House

**T**HIS CABINET IS for storing keys and other items you might need going out the door, such as a dog leash, a flashlight, or a pair of gloves. I designed the cabinet to look like a small house with a simple board door complete with a working doorknob latch. Keys are means through which we open doors and enter other spaces. Like a house, keys are a symbol of safety and security.

So much of modern life is virtual, its workings mysterious. This small cabinet is made so you can see clearly how it works. The pins securing the joints are made obvious, as are other details—the pivoting door latch and the visible rabbet joint holding up the shelf.

I like to work with American hardwoods, and most of the lumber I use comes from my own state of Arkansas. Occasionally, a small quantity of more unusual species comes my way. This black locust seemed just right for this key cabinet, but you can make your version from any kind of hardwood.

# Key house

This small cabinet uses fairly simple joinery. The sides of the cabinet are joined to the bottom and shelf with a dadoed rabbet joint that's easy to cut on the tablesaw. The "gables" are attached to the sides with through dowels, as is the "roof."

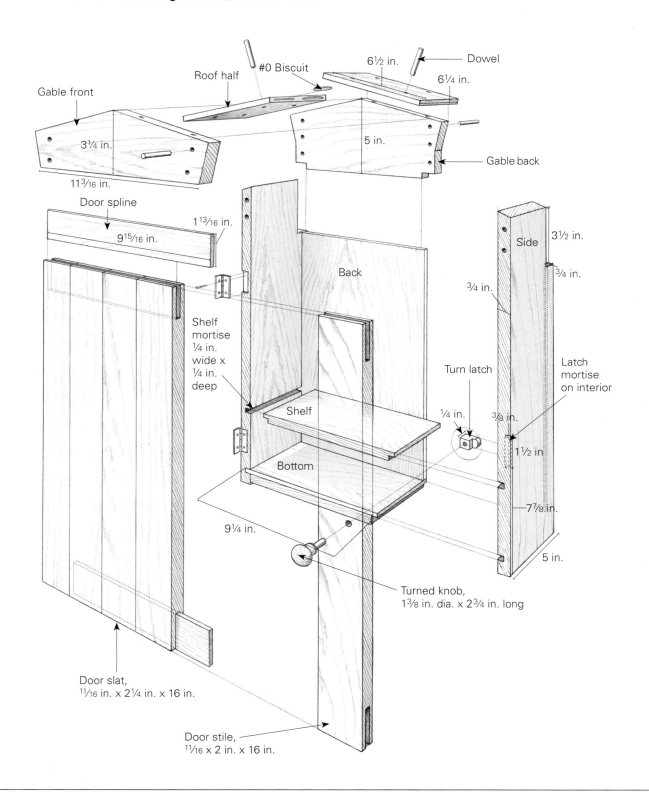

Gable front

Roof half

#0 Biscuit

6½ in.

Dowel

6¼ in.

3¼ in.

5 in.

Gable back

11³⁄₁₆ in.

Door spline

1¹³⁄₁₆ in.

9¹⁵⁄₁₆ in.

Side

3½ in.

¾ in.

Back

¾ in.

Shelf mortise ¼ in. wide x ¼ in. deep

Shelf

Turn latch

Latch mortise on interior

¼ in.

⅜ in.

1½ in.

Bottom

7⅞ in.

9¼ in.

5 in.

Turned knob, 1⅜ in. dia. x 2¾ in. long

Door slat, ¹¹⁄₁₆ in. x 2¼ in. x 16 in.

Door stile, ¹¹⁄₁₆ x 2 in. x 16 in.

# MATERIALS FOR KEY HOUSE

| QUANTITY | PART | SIZE | NOTES |
|---|---|---|---|
| 1 | Front gable | $\frac{7}{8}$ in. x $3\frac{1}{4}$ in. x $11\frac{1}{4}$ in.* | Back locust |
| 1 | Back gable | $\frac{3}{4}$ in. x 5 in. x $11\frac{1}{4}$ in.* | Black locust |
| 2 | Sides | $\frac{3}{4}$ in. x 5 in. x 18 in. | Black locust |
| 1 | Bottom | $\frac{3}{4}$ in. x 5 in. x $9\frac{1}{4}$ in. | Black locust |
| 1 | Shelf | $\frac{1}{2}$ in. x $4\frac{3}{4}$ in. x $9\frac{1}{4}$ in. | Black locust |
| 2 | Roof sections | $\frac{5}{8}$ in. x $6\frac{1}{4}$ in. x $6\frac{1}{2}$ in. | Black locust |
| 1 | Back | $\frac{1}{4}$ in. x $9\frac{1}{4}$ in. x $13\frac{7}{8}$ in. | Baltic-birch plywood |
| 2 | Door stiles | $\frac{11}{16}$ in. x 2 in. x 16 in. | Black locust |
| 3 | Door slats | $\frac{11}{16}$ in. x $2\frac{1}{4}$ in. x 16 in. | Black locust |
| 2 | Door splines | $\frac{1}{4}$ in. x $1\frac{13}{16}$ in. x $9\frac{15}{16}$ in. | Black locust |
| 2 | Biscuits | #0 | |
| 1 | Knob | $1\frac{3}{8}$ in. dia. x $2\frac{3}{4}$-in. long | Cherry |
| 1 | Latch | $\frac{3}{4}$ x $1\frac{3}{8}$ in. x $1\frac{3}{8}$ in. | Cherry |
| 18 | Dowels | $\frac{1}{4}$ in. dia x $1\frac{3}{4}$ in. | Contrasting hardwood |
| 1 pr. | Hinges | $\frac{7}{8}$ in. x $1\frac{1}{2}$ in. | Ace Hardware #5299755 |
| 4 | Shoulder hooks | 1 in. | Hardware store item |
| 8 | Shoulder hooks | $\frac{3}{4}$ in. | Hardware store item |
| 14 | Wire brads | #18 x $\frac{5}{8}$ in. | |

*Size before cutting to shape.

## TABLESAW BLADES FOR JOINERY

For the tablesaw joinery for this project and others in the book, I use a special grind blade that has a square-topped cut. Many blades, both crosscut and rip, leave a small V of uncut stock at the center of the cut because they are angled at the top edge of the tooth. The blade I use is a Forrest Woodworker II with #1 OD special grind. You'll also find this feature on some combination blades. Look for blades that have a flat-top grind (FTG).

A FTG-tooth blade will enable you to make cuts and widen them as needed for a groove, dado, or other joint without having to change to a dado blade. Changing blades requires time and setup. The cleaner cut from an FTG-tooth blade is especially important on exposed joinery, where the meeting parts will be visible on the outside.

# Build the cabinet box

**MILL THE LUMBER FOR THE CABINET BOX** to thickness and cut the parts to length and width. First flatten one face of the stock on the jointer. Then plane it to thickness. Use a jointer to square one edge. Rip the stock to width and length. Use a crosscut sled on the tablesaw with a stop block to make certain that paired parts are the same length. Cut the bottom and shelf to length, but leave the sides a bit long so that you can cut an angle at the top later.

**BEGIN THE RABBET** on each end of the bottom and fixed shelf, using the tablesaw and sled. The stop block is set to form a rabbet ⅜ in. deep.

**CUT THE DADOES FOR BOTTOM AND SHELF.** Make the first cut where the bottom of the groove begins. Then widen the groove to ¼ in. by moving the stop block ⅛ in. closer to the blade.

**1.** Cut the dadoes for the shelf and the bottom. For the bottom, set the stop block so the blade will cut 1 in. from the end of the stock. Make cuts on the insides of each cabinet side and then adjust the stop block by ⅛ in., bringing it closer to the blade for the next cut **(PHOTO A)**. This will widen the groove to ¼ in. For the shelf, begin the cut 5⅛ in. up from the bottom edge. Move the stop block closer to the blade to widen the cut to ¼ in.

**2.** Cut the shoulder for the rabbet on the ends of the shelf and bottom. First, make cuts with the sled and stop block ⅜ in. from the end of the stock **(PHOTO B)**. Note that although the shelf and bottom

**COMPLETE THE RABBET.** Set the fence ¼ in. from the blade. Stand the stock on end against the fence. A feather board holds the wood tightly against the fence.

are different thicknesses, the tongues are all ¼ in. thick, so you'll have to adjust the blade height.

**3.** Set the tablesaw fence so that it is ¼ in. from the blade and set the blade height at ⅜ in. Then cut the stock with it standing on end against the fence **(PHOTO C)**. To make this cut, you will need a zero-clearance insert to support the stock during the cut. As an alternative, use the setup in the previous step **(PHOTO B)**, and make additional cuts, pulling the stock away from the stop block until the short tenon is formed.

# Make and fit the gables

**1.** Cut a ¾-in.-deep space at the back of the sides, from the top edge to 3½ in. down for the back gable. Nibble the stock in ⅛-in. increments with the blade set at a ¾-in. height. Set the stop block so the last cut will be 3½ in. down from the top. Start at the end and keep cutting until the stock reaches the stop block **(PHOTO D)**.

**CUT A NOTCH FOR THE BACK GABLE.** Nibble away the stock ⅛ in. at a time until the stock reaches the stock block, which is set to limit the cut to 3½ in. down from the top edge.

**CUT THE 15° ANGLE** to form the roofline on each gable. Use a precision miter gauge. Clamp a stop block to the miter gauge to hold the stock in a fixed position in relation to the blade.

**CUT THE TOP OF THE SIDES TO A 15° ANGLE. A trial fit of the back gable will give you the precise location for the cut.**

**2.** Use the same technique to cut a notch on each end of the back gable (stretcher). Set the blade height at ⅜ in., and set the stop block 1½ in. from the outside of the cut to begin shaping the back stretcher to fit the sides. Again, make the first cuts at the end and keep cutting until the stock reaches the stop block for your final cut.

**3.** Cut 15° angles at the top of each gable to form the roofline. Clamp a wider board to the miter gauge to help hold the part securely while you make the cut **(PHOTO E)**. To make this miter gauge accessory, screw a clamping board to a piece of plywood wide enough to hold the stock securely without twisting in the cut. Clamp the accessory board to the miter gauge to serve as both a stop block and stabilizer for the cut.

**4.** Next cut the sides to a 15° angle at the top. Tilt the blade to 15°. Then use the miter gauge to make the cuts with the inside surface facing up. Use a stop block to make certain that both sides are precisely the same length **(PHOTO F)**. One way to ensure this is to set a stop block at the end of the miter gauge before you make the cut in one side. Then just place the end of the second side against the block to make the second cut.

**ROUT RABBETS ON THE INSIDE BACK EDGES** of the sides for the back panel. I use a stop on the router table fence to keep the cut from going all the way along the back edge.

**ROUT THE MATCHING RABBET** in the back gable with the part standing on edge.

**5.** Cut the rabbets. Use a ½-in.-dia. or larger straight-cut router bit in the router table to cut rabbets on the edges of the sides, bottom, and back stretcher. Set the router bit height to ⅜ in. and set the fence so that the bit protrudes ¼ in. from the edge of the fence. Rout the sides and bottom with the inside faces flat down on the router table **(PHOTO G)**.

**6.** Rout the bottom edge of the back gable to match the rabbet on the sides. Stand the gable on edge, bottom side down for this cut **(PHOTO H)**.

**7.** Drill the dowel holes in the front and back gables. Use a ¼-in. drill bit and set the fence on the drill press 1 in. from the center of the drill bit. Set the drill depth so it passes all the way through the stock **(PHOTO I)**.

**8.** Cut a notch on each end of the back stretcher. Raise the blade on the tablesaw for a cut 1¾ in. above the sled table. Set the stop block to make a cut ½ in. from the edge **(PHOTO J)**. Then mark a line from the top inside edge of the cut you just made to the top corner of the stock on each end.

**DRILL ¼-IN. HOLES FOR THE DOWELS** in the front and back gables 1 in. on center from both sides. Set the drill press to drill through the stock.

**BEGIN TO SHAPE THE BACK GABLE** on the tablesaw using a crosscut sled and stop block.

# Gable detail

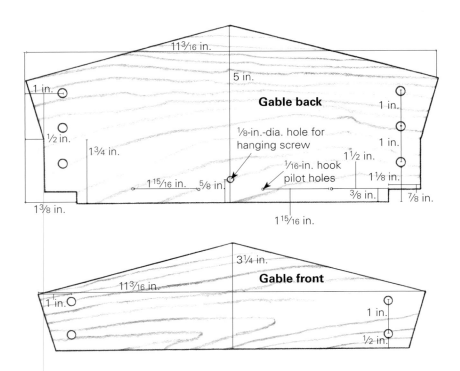

11³⁄₁₆ in.

5 in.

**Gable back**

1 in.

1 in.

1 in.

⅛-in.-dia. hole for hanging screw

1½ in.

1 in.

1½ in.

¹⁄₁₆-in. hook pilot holes

1⅛ in.

1³⁄₄ in.

1¹⁵⁄₁₆ in.

⅝ in.

⅜ in.

⅞ in.

1⅜ in.

½ in.

1¹⁵⁄₁₆ in.

3¼ in.

**Gable front**

11³⁄₁₆ in.

1 in.

1 in.

½ in.

**CUT THE ANGLE** at the ends of the gable on the bandsaw.

**DRILL A ¹⁄₈-IN. HOLE** through the back gable for the screw to hang the cabinet. Use a countersink bit to shape the hole to fit a flat-head screw.

**9.** Cut the angle on the bandsaw (**PHOTO K**). Lay out a 75° angle on each end of the front gable from ½ in. in from the end of the bottom edge to the upper corner. Cut this shape on the bandsaw.

**10.** Drill the ⅛-in. hanger hole centered, ⅝ in. up from the bottom edge of the back gable (**PHOTO L**). Also drill ¹⁄₁₆-in. pilot holes for the shoulder hooks as shown in the drawing above.

# Make the roof and prepare for assembly

**CUT A 15° ANGLE** where the two roof sections intersect. Cut the sections to length with a crosscut sled.

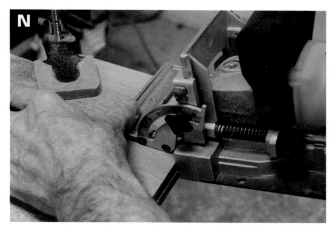

**CUT #0 BISCUIT SLOTS** at a 15° angle where the two roof sections meet.

**1.** Tilt the tablesaw blade 15°. Make the angle cuts on the stock where the two halves will join using a miter gauge **(PHOTO M)**.

**2.** Then use the crosscut sled on the tablesaw to trim the two roof halves to length. Using a stop block to control length of cut will ensure that both halves are the same length.

**3.** Next drill the ¼-in. holes in the roof sections to allow for attaching them to the front and back stretchers. Refer to the drawing below for the exact positioning of the holes.

**4.** Use a biscuit joiner to make slots in the angled end of each roof section for #0 biscuits **(PHOTO N)**. Set the biscuit joiner fence to 15° (off from 90°). Mark the centerlines for each biscuit about 1¾ in. from the front and back edge of the stock.

**5.** Use clear plastic packaging tape to hold the parts together at the top after you have applied glue to the edges and put biscuits in place. Then apply pressure from the ends to close the joint tight on the biscuits, by using blocks of wood clamped to the

## Roof detail

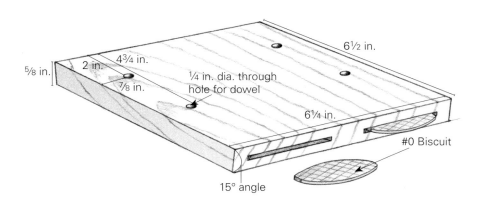

6½ in.

5/8 in.

2 in.

4¾ in.

7/8 in.

¼ in. dia. through hole for dowel

6¼ in.

15° angle

#0 Biscuit

USE TAPE TO SECURE THE TWO ROOF HALVES while the glue dries. Blocks on each end serve in lieu of clamps to close the joint on the underside.

ROUT A ³/₈-IN.-DIA. GROOVE for the turn key with a plunge router and straight bit. Make the cut in multiple passes.

workbench. Clamp one block in position, and apply pressure to the second block as you close the joint. Then clamp the second block in position. Wait until the glue has set before removing the clamps and the tape **(PHOTO O)**.

**6.** Cut a 1½-in.-long groove in the left side (or right if you want to reverse the door opening) for the latch. Use a plunge router and ³/₈-in.-dia. spiral cutter. Set the router fence to control the distance from the edge

at ³/₈ in. and set the router depth at ³/₈ in. Begin the groove 7⅞ in. up from bottom edge of the side. Make start and stop lines to guide where to plunge into the cut and where to lift the router to end the cut. Rout the groove in several passes rather than attempting to make the cut in a single pass **(PHOTO P)**.

**7.** Lay out and cut the hinge mortises as shown on pp. 17–19.

## Assemble the cabinet

ASSEMBLE THE SIDES, SHELF, AND BOTTOM. Tightly clamp the parts together as the glue sets. Check to make certain the cabinet is square.

To attach the front and back stretchers and roof to the sides, you will need ¼-in.-dia. dowels, which you can buy at a hardware or lumber store. Woodworking suppliers offer dowels in different hardwood species. You can use either matching or contrasting hardwoods depending on how much you want to emphasize the exposed joinery look.

**1.** Apply glue inside the grooves cut into the sides, then align the bottom and fixed shelf in position. Use bar clamps to pull the parts tight, and use a square to check that the assembly is held square as the glue sets **(PHOTO Q)**.

**2.** Sand the ends of the dowels before assembly. Then use a hand-held drill and ¼-in. bit to finish the holes for installing the dowels. Start with the back gable since the notches cut in it make it easiest to clamp securely in relation to the sides. I use a thin block of wood as my drill stop, so that each hole will be drilled to the exact depth required for the length of the dowels **(PHOTO R)**.

**3.** Spread glue in the dowel holes and use a block of wood to cushion and direct the hammer blows as you drive the dowels in place.

**4.** Use clamps to secure the roof in place as you prepare to drill and drive holes for attaching it to the front and back stretchers. I use a thin bead of glue on the top edges of the stretchers before clamping the roof in place and then wait for the glue to set before drilling the holes and driving the dowels in place. Remember to put a bit of glue in each dowel hole for a permanent fit **(PHOTO S)**.

**5.** After the stretchers and roof are in place, lay a thin bead of glue in the rabbet at the back and nail the sanded back panel in place using 18-gauge ⅝-in. brads.

**DRILL TO COMPLETE** the dowel holes in the cabinet sides. Clamp the sides and back gable into alignment, then use a stop block on the bit to drill to a uniform depth.

**GLUE AND CLAMP THE TOP** to the cabinet sides, front, and back. Just a thin line of glue is needed.

# Build the doors

**THE INSPIRATION FOR THE DOOR WAS** traditional-style board-and-batten doors, which have boards (battens) nailed to the back of the uprights. Instead, I concealed the "batten" and made it into a spline milled to fit a slot at each end of each board. The door has five upright lapped boards similar to lapped siding.

**1.** Arrange and mark the boards and mark their position on the front face to keep track of where you should be cutting. Note that only one edge of the stiles is lapped.

**CUT THE SHOULDER OF THE HALF-LAP JOINTS** on each side of the door slats and on the inside edges of the door stiles. On the slats, make the cut on one face, then flip the board over and cut on the opposite face.

**2.** Begin by cutting the shoulder of the lapped joint on the edges **(PHOTO A)**. Use the tablesaw to make a cut ¼ in. from the edge, halfway through the

**B**

COMPLETE THE LAP JOINT by adjusting the fence and blade height and cutting the stock on edge.

**C**

USE A TENONING JIG TO CUT THE SLOTS in each end of the door slats.

thickness of the door stock. (If the stock is milled precisely to $^{11}\!/_{16}$ in., the blade height will be set at $^{11}\!/_{32}$ in.)

**3.** Raise the blade height to $^{1}\!/_{4}$ in. and reset the fence to cut at $^{11}\!/_{32}$ in. Turn the stock on edge and make the cut to remove the waste **(PHOTO B)**. Use a featherboard to keep the stock tight to the fence.

**4.** Use a tenoning jig (see p. 41) on the tablesaw to cut the slots for the splines **(PHOTO C)**. Set the blade height to $1^{3}\!/_{4}$ in. Note that the slot is off-center. The distance from the front face to the slot is $^{3}\!/_{16}$ in. The distance from the back of the slot to the back face is $^{1}\!/_{4}$ in. Choose which will be the front and back face on each piece and keep the back face consistently against the body of the jig.

**5.** Mill the splines to thickness to fit the slot ($^{1}\!/_{4}$ in.) and cut to length and width.

**6.** Rout the edges of each board and sand the edges where the boards will intersect **(PHOTO D)**.

When cutting stock on edge, use a featherboard to keep the stock tight to the fence. Your cuts will be more precise and you'll have better control of the stock.

**7.** To assemble the doors, start with two opposite corners and two splines. Spread glue on the ends of each spline, being careful to glue only those surfaces that will fit inside the grooves cut in the door boards. Use a square to make certain that the two opposite corners are assembled square. Use a C-clamp and blocks of wood to cushion and distribute clamping pressure as the glue sets. After the glue has dried, assemble the remaining parts. Spread glue on the exposed ends and pull the door parts into a complete whole. Before using C-clamps to clamp the corner joints, make sure the assembly is square and that the boards are spaced to attain the full 10-in. width. There should be about a $^{1}\!/_{32}$-in. space between each board to allow for possible expansion during periods of high humidity **(PHOTO E)**.

**8.** After the glue has set, remove the clamps and trim the splines flush to the surrounding edges.

**D**

ROUT THE EDGES OF THE DOOR SLATS with a $^{1}\!/_{8}$-in. roundover bit. Adjust the height to rout the "short" side.

**ASSEMBLE THE CENTER PARTS** of the door, and after spreading glue on the top and bottom, pull the parts into position and clamp the slots tight on the strips.

**9.** Lay out and cut the door hinge mortises as shown on pp. 17–19. Note that because the door overlaps the cabinet, the hinge is on the rear face of the door instead of on the edge of the door.

**10.** You can buy a pull from your hardware store or woodworking supply company. Or turn a knob on the lathe. After turning the knob to the desired shape, I use a stick cut with an opening of ½ in. or a ½-in. open-end wrench as my guide for getting the shaft trimmed to the right diameter **(PHOTO F)**.

**11.** Use the drill press with a ½-in. bit to drill holes all the way through the door and to a depth of ⅝ in. on the turn latch **(PHOTO G)**.

**12.** To make the turn latch, cut a piece of long stock to a dimension of ¾ in. × 1⅜ in. and cut one end to form a ⅜-in. × ⅜-in. tenon the full width on one end. Then, after shaping the curved end on the sander and drilling the hole for the knob end to fit, cut the latch part to final length. Before gluing the latch to the knob shaft, check its operation and refine its final fit to make certain that it will open and lock when the knob is turned.

**13.** Sand the cabinet and apply the finish of your choice. I used two coats of hand-rubbed Danish oil.

**14.** Install the hinges and hang the door as described on p. 19.

## Knob and latch detail

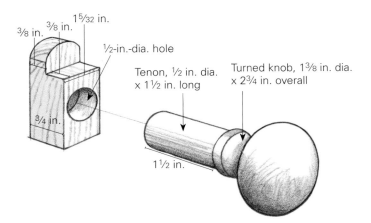

3/8 in.   3/8 in.   1 5/32 in.   ½-in.-dia. hole   3/4 in.

Tenon, ½ in. dia. × 1½ in. long   Turned knob, 1⅜ in. dia. × 2¾ in. overall   1½ in.

**USE THE LATHE TO TURN A KNOB.** Then form a ½-in.-dia. tenon. Use a measurement strip (shown here) or open-end wrench to check that the proper diameter is achieved.

**DRILL HOLES** in the latch and door for the knob. Use a ½-in.-dia. bit in the drill press.

# Panel-Door Spice Cabinet

**T**HE PROTOTYPE for this spice cabinet was a gift for my wife not long after we married. I inscribed the inside of the left door, "Happy Birthday, Jean 1985." My wife is a librarian, so of course she wanted a cabinet in which the spice containers could be arranged alphabetically. I also wanted the cabinet to be able to hold common-sized spice jars. For over a quarter century, that first cabinet has added visual beauty to our kitchen, kept it neater, and made our cooking more enjoyable. This project is proof that the practical can be beautiful. Building it will give you an opportunity to learn how to use biscuit joinery, which is a quick and efficient method of building small cabinets. In this chapter you'll also learn how to rout hinge mortises using a shopmade template. And you'll see how subtle enhancements, like small chamfers in the frame-and-panel door, can have a big design impact.

# Panel-door spice cabinet

This spice cabinet is full of details that give it visual appeal, including the cathedral door panels. Use a contrasting wood for the door panels for a completely different look. Note that the door rails and panels are trimmed to final size during construction.

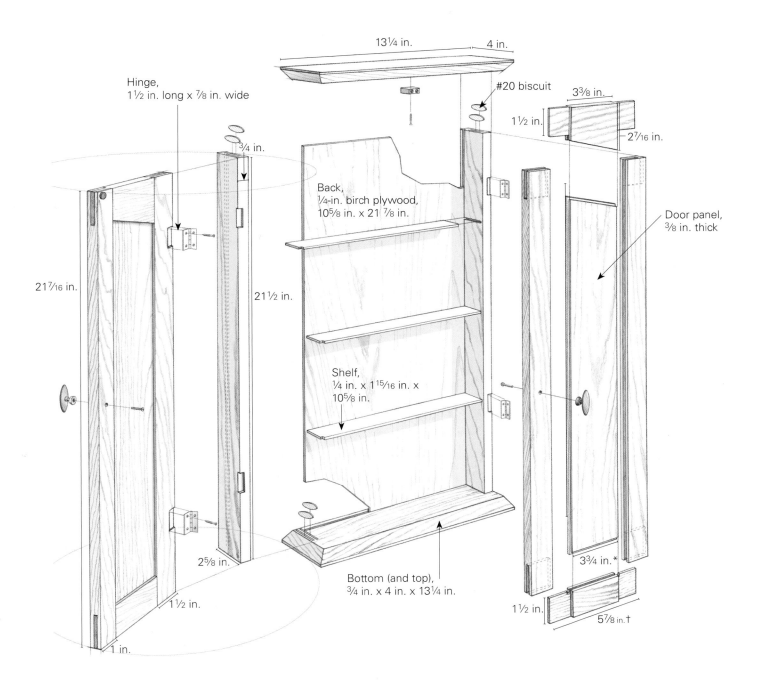

13¼ in.

4 in.

Hinge, 1½ in. long x ⅞ in. wide

#20 biscuit

3⅜ in.

1½ in.

2⁷⁄₁₆ in.

¾ in.

Back, ¼-in. birch plywood, 10⅝ in. x 21⅞ in.

Door panel, ⅜ in. thick

21⁷⁄₁₆ in.

21½ in.

Shelf, ¼ in. x 1¹⁵⁄₁₆ in. x 10⅝ in.

2⅝ in.

3¾ in. *

1½ in.

Bottom (and top), ¾ in. x 4 in. x 13¼ in.

1½ in.

1 in.

5⅞ in.†

*Trimmed to fit actual frame opening
†Inside tenon trimmed after assembly

## MATERIALS

| QUANTITY | PART | SIZE | NOTES |
|---|---|---|---|
| 2 | Top and Bottom | ¾ in. x 4 in. x 13¼ in. | Cherry |
| 2 | Sides | ¾ in. x 2⅝ in. x 21½ in. | Cherry |
| 2 | Outer door stiles | ⅝ in. x 1½ in. x 21$\frac{7}{16}$ in. | Cherry |
| 2 | Inner door stiles | ⅝ in. x 1 in. x 21$\frac{7}{16}$ in. | Cherry |
| 2 | Bottom door rails | ⅝ in. x 1½ in. x 6⅜ in.* | Cherry |
| 2 | Top door rails | ⅝ in. x 2$\frac{7}{16}$ in. x 6⅜ in.* | Cherry |
| 2 | Door panels | ⅜ in. x 3¾ in. x 18⅝ in.† | Cherry or contrasting hardwood‡ |
| 1 | Back | ¼ in. x 10⅝ x 21⅞ in. | Baltic-birch plywood |
| 3 | Shelves | ¼ in. x 1$\frac{15}{16}$ in. x 10⅝ in. | Cherry |
| 1 | Catch block | ⅝ in. x 1½ in. x 1$\frac{15}{16}$ in. | Cherry |
| 1 | Hanger | ⅜ in. x 2⅝ in. x 10¼ in. | Cherry |
| 1 | Wall hanger | ⅜ in. x 2⅝ in. x 10$\frac{3}{16}$ in. | Cherry |
| 2 pr. | Brass hinges | 1½ in. x ⅞ in. | Ace Hardware #5299755 |
| 8 | Biscuits | #20 | |
| 2 | Cabinet pulls | $\frac{7}{16}$ in. x 1½ in. x ⅞ in. | Amerock® #BP4476-FB |
| 2 | Door magnets | | Woodcraft® #145289 |

*Trimmed to final length after assembly. †Size before cutting the $\frac{3}{16}$-in. x $\frac{3}{16}$-in. tongue on the end and sides. Final size determined after fitting within door frame. ‡Resawn and book-matched from 4/4 stock.

# Cut the biscuit joints

**BISCUIT JOINERY IS A QUICK AND EFFECTIVE** way to make small cabinets. The biscuit joiner cuts half-round shaped slots with a small circular blade. Compressed wood wafers or biscuits fit into the slot. When a biscuit comes in contact with glue, the moisture causes it to swell, creating a tight joint.

**1.** Cut the parts to length on the tablesaw. Use a crosscut sled and stop block to make certain that parts of the same type (sides, top, and bottom) are sized to equal lengths.

**2.** Set up the fence of the biscuit joiner to cut slots in the sides on both ends. Position the biscuits at least $\frac{3}{16}$ in. from the inside surface of the cabinet to allow for the groove that will be cut for the back panel **(PHOTO A)**. I prefer to use two biscuits for extra strength, though one would suffice.

**3.** Reset the biscuit joiner fence to allow for the overhang at the edges of the top and bottom and cut the slots **(PHOTO B)**.

**CUT THE BISCUIT SLOTS INTO THE ENDS** of the cabinet sides. Cut the first biscuit slot on each end of each side, then adjust the fence to cut the slots for the second biscuits.

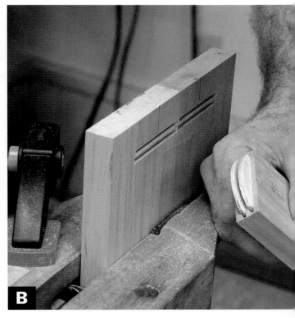

**CLAMP THE TOP AND BOTTOM VERTICALLY** and adjust the biscuit joiner fence to position the biscuits so that the top and bottom overlap the sides. Placing the top and bottom side by side gives additional support to the biscuit joiner during this operation.

# Fit the back

**SET THE FENCE SO THE GROOVE WILL BE** cut ⅜ in. from the back edge of each side, top and bottom. Note that the groove is positioned to end at the inside biscuit slot, so the biscuits won't interfere with the back during assembly.

**1.** Mount a ¼-in. straight bit in the router table to rout a ³⁄₁₆-in.-deep groove for the back panel. To rout the top and bottom, use stop blocks clamped on the router table fence to control the travel of the workpiece to prevent the groove from showing. **(PHOTO A).**

**ROUT A GROOVE** across the inside of the top and bottom for the back panel. Use stop blocks to control the travel of the workpiece, and use the biscuit slots as a guide to set the stop blocks.

**THE GROOVE IN THE SIDES** is a through cut, so you can remove the stop blocks from the router table.

**CUT THE BALTIC-BIRCH** plywood for the back to size.

**2.** To rout the groove in the cabinet sides, remove the stop blocks and make a through cut (**PHOTO B**).

**3.** Cut the cabinet back to size using the tablesaw. I use ¼-in. Baltic-birch plywood. On occasion, the plywood will be slightly too thick, in which case you can trim the edges or slightly widen the grooves cut in the top, bottom, and sides to match (**PHOTO C**).

# Make the shelves

**LAY OUT AND ROUT THE GROOVES** on both sides at the same time to ensure correct alignment. The pencil mark on the fence indicates the position the router bit will cut. Place a mark on the cabinet sides. Then align the mark on the jig to it.

**BECAUSE THIS IS A SPICE CABINET WITH** fixed spacing for each shelf, rout the cabinet sides for shelves to fit. Use a distance of 5³⁄₁₆ in. for equally spaced shelves, or measure the heights of the jars of your favorite spice brands for more space-efficient variable spacing. (You can also make adjustable shelves, as shown on p. 8.) To speed the layout of fixed shelves, make a simple jig to guide the router from a piece of ½-in. plywood, attached with screws to a straight piece of wood.

**1.** Mark the shelf locations on the cabinet sides (**PHOTO A**). Note that the pencil mark on the jig fence corresponds with the position of the router bit when the base is held against the plywood guide, so all you have to do is slide the guide to align the

**B**

**ROUT THE SHELF dadoes.** Move the plunge router from left to right between start and stop lines penciled on each side. Make this cut in two passes. First, take a shallow cut. Then return the router to its starting point, lower the bit to full depth, and rout from left to right.

mark with the one for the shelf location and then rout between the start and stop lines you've penciled onto the cabinet sides.

**2.** Mount a ³⁄₈-in. router bit in a plunge router. Set the full plunge depth to ³⁄₁₆ in. Hold the router base against the plywood guide as you rout from left to right **(PHOTO B)**. Don't try to cut to full depth in one pass. Lower the bit into the work for a partial-depth cut and make the first pass. Raise the bit, then when you are at your starting point, plunge to full depth while moving the router from left to right.

**WORK SMART**

Another option would be to cut the groove closer to the front end of the sides and round the fronts of each shelf using a ¹⁄₈-in.-radius roundover bit in the router table. I prefer the option shown as it requires less precision on the width of the routed grooves.

**C**

**MAKE A SMALL CUT AT THE FRONT** of each shelf to conceal the routed grooves. Plane the shelves to fit the groove, then make the cut shown, or chisel the grooves square, or round the shelves to fit the groove using a ¹⁄₈-in. roundover bit in the router table.

**3.** Plane the shelf stock to final thickness to fit the grooves. Cut the shelves to final width and length. Cut a notch in the front at both ends of the shelves to hide the routed grooves **(PHOTO C)**.

# Shape the top and bottom

**ON A SMALL CABINET LIKE THIS, THE STOCK** used for the top and bottom could have been overbearing. Beveling these parts makes them appear lighter and more refined. In addition to the 30° bevel on the inside faces of the top and bottom, I add a smaller ⅛-in. bevel to the outer faces.

**1.** Set the tablesaw blade to 30°, keeping it as low as possible to make the cut. Use a tenoning jig (see the facing page) to hold the parts while you cut the short edges. Set the position of the cut so it lies outside the area occupied by the biscuits. The visible flat area remaining after the angled cut will be approximately ⁵⁄₁₆ in. **(PHOTO A)**.

**USE A TENONING JIG ON THE TABLESAW** to hold the top and bottom as the edges are shaped. I have the saw set at a 30° angle, and the fence set so that the blade avoids the space where the sides will fit.

On this step, I always make a test cut first in scrap stock of the same thickness so I don't mess up the nearly completed parts. Cutting on scrap stock of the same thickness can help you to avoid mistakes. While we all learn from our mistakes, woodworking is more fun when you don't waste your project wood.

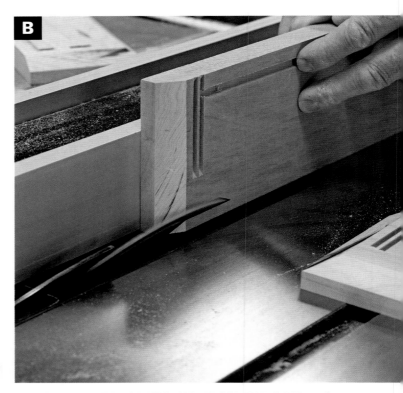

**REMOVE THE TENONING JIG FROM THE SAW,** and move the fence over ¾ in. toward the blade to make the angle cut across the front of the top and bottom.

**2.** The cut on the long edge will be made bearing against the fence. Adjust the fence position so that the cut meets the top and bottom at the same point on the corners as in the previous cut. Make test cuts and keep the tablesaw blade as low as you can to make the cut **(PHOTO B)**.

**3.** Use a sanding block to sand all the cut surfaces and edges of the top and bottom before assembly. A sanding block will be more effective than a power sander and will help prevent rounding the surfaces by mistake.

Use scrap cabinet-grade plywood to build a simple tenoning jig that slides along the rip fence on your tablesaw. The location of the cut is set by adjusting the distance of the fence from the blade. The crucial dimensions are the height and width of your fence. You want the jig to fit snuggly over the fence but slide freely.

Measure the height of the fence, then set the distance between the fence and the blade to equal that dimension. Set the blade height on the tablesaw about one-half the thickness of the plywood (in this case ⅜ in.). Make the first cut on the slide at the back of the fence and the other on the piece forming the face of the jig. Gradually widen the cut on each piece by moving the fence in small increments until a piece of plywood will fit in the groove. You want an exact fit, so work up to it in very small increments (see photo below left). Cut a piece of hardwood to form the vertical backing piece and use the same series of steps to fit it into a ⅜-in.-deep groove.

Next, cut a piece of plywood to fit between the two. Then use screws to attach the front and back to the center. If the assembled jig is too tight, use card stock as shims to widen the space. By adding or subtracting thicknesses of paper, you can adjust to a perfect fit (see photo below right).

Shape the parts so that they fit comfortably when you grip them for use. I also cut away portions of the face so that I can position clamps to hold the stock to be tenoned. Add a block of wood to make certain that the face of the jig is square to the body.

Screw rather than glue the parts together. That way, you can take the jig apart to make adjustments or to replace the vertical backing piece as it becomes worn.

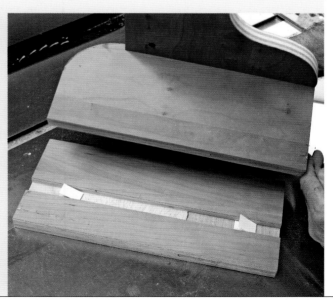

# Assemble the carcase

**BEFORE ASSEMBLY, SAND THE SHELVES** and inside surfaces of the cabinet. Always do a test-fit before gluing any parts just to make certain you won't encounter any obstructions during the actual assembly. Be prepared with enough clamps of the right type and size and be familiar with how each clamp works.

**1.** Apply glue in each of the biscuit slots **(PHOTO A)**. Be sparing with the glue or the excess will overflow into the interior of the cabinet.

**2.** Assemble the parts around the back panel. Clamp from the front and back over the location of the biscuits **(PHOTO B)**. Check that the cabinet is square by measuring corner to corner. If the measurement is exactly the same in each direction, it's square. You can also use a square in the corners.

**A**

**APPLY GLUE IN THE BISCUIT SLOTS** and then insert the biscuits.

**B**

**PULL THE JOINTS TOGETHER** with clamps after the biscuits and glue are in place.

# Make the door components

**A**

**LAY OUT THE PARTS FOR THE DOORS** and mark the stiles and rails in the position they will be assembled.

**FOR SMALL PROJECTS LIKE THIS CABINET,** bridle joints are attractive and strong enough to last for generations, and unlike dowels or biscuits, don't depend on stock thickness.

**1.** Plane all the wood down to ⅝ in. thick so the doors will be lightweight. Cut the parts to size and lay them out to get the most pleasing grain pattern.

**2.** Mark the parts with a pencil to identify their relationship to one another and to indicate the face side and the inside **(PHOTO A)**.

# Cut the door joinery

**1.** Cut the bridles in the stiles on a tablesaw outfitted with a blade with flat-top-grind (FTG) teeth. Use a tenoning jig to accurately position the cut and support the workpiece. Make the first cut ³⁄₁₆ in. from the front face on both ends of all the stiles. Then widen the bridle opening to ³⁄₁₆ in. by adjusting the tenoning jig. Keep the front face to the jig for all cuts **(PHOTO B)**. Note that the rear leg of the bridle is ¼ in. thick.

**2.** Cut the tenons on the tablesaw using the same setup. Lay out the cut using the bridles in the stiles as a template, but remember to cut on the outside of the line **(PHOTO C)** and that the tenon is offset from center. The distance to the front face is ³⁄₁₆ in.; from the back, it's ¼ in.

**3.** To cut the shoulders of the tenon, use a cross-cut sled and a special stop block to prevent trapping the cut-off between the stop and the blade. **(PHOTOS D, E)**. Set the stop block to cut 1½-in.-long tenons on each end. Set the blade to cut the front shoulder on all the rails at ³⁄₁₆ in. Then turn over the stock and raise the blade to cut the ¼-in. rear shoulders.

**CUT THE BRIDLE** with a tenoning jig. With the face side of each stile facing the tenoning jig, make a ⅛-in.-wide cut, then adjust the fence to widen the cut to ³⁄₁₆ in.

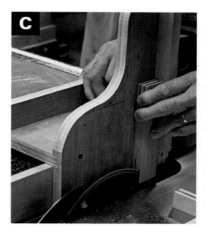

**TO LAY OUT** the rail tenons, use the bridle in the stile for the setup. Cut on the waste side of the transferred line. Make your first cut with the face side against the jig. Then move the fence to cut the other side, again with the face side of the stock against the body of the jig.

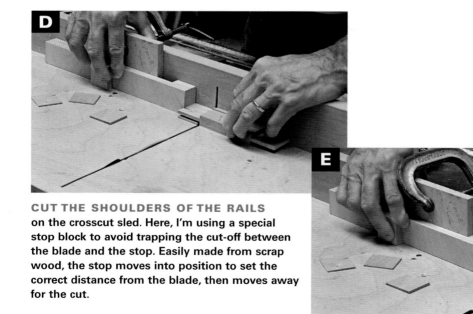

**CUT THE SHOULDERS OF THE RAILS** on the crosscut sled. Here, I'm using a special stop block to avoid trapping the cut-off between the blade and the stop. Easily made from scrap wood, the stop moves into position to set the correct distance from the blade, then moves away for the cut.

**F**

MAKE A CUT ON EACH END of the upper rails to correspond to the height of the bridle on the door stiles.

**G**

CUT THE RAIL TENONS to width using the sliding stop block to position the cut.

**4.** Finish cutting the tenons of the top rails. First, stand the horizontal top stretcher on end and cut the tenon to a width of 1½ in. from the top **(PHOTO F)**.

**5.** Reposition the workpiece. Use the sliding stop block as shown in the previous step to complete the shoulder **(PHOTO G)**.

**6.** Lay out the angle on each top rail as shown in the drawing below.

**7.** Make the cut on the bandsaw **(PHOTO H)**. Smooth the cut with sandpaper or a handplane.

**H**

MAKE THE ANGLED CUT at the bottom of the top rails on the bandsaw.

## Top rail detail

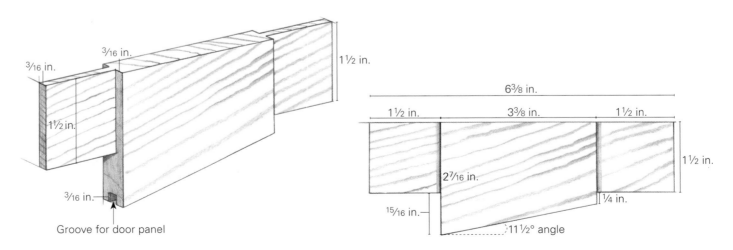

3/16 in.
3/16 in.
3/16 in.
1½ in.
1½ in.
3/16 in.
Groove for door panel

1½ in.
6⅜ in.
1½ in.
3⅜ in.
1½ in.
2⁷/16 in.
1½ in.
¼ in.
15/16 in.
11½° angle

**ROUT THE GROOVES** in the stiles and rails for the front panels. Set a stop block before routing the bottom rails to stop the cut so it doesn't show on the through tenon.

**WIDEN THE GROOVES** to ³⁄₁₆ in. by moving the fence away from the cut and making a second pass with each part on the router table.

**8.** Rout a ³⁄₁₆-in.-deep groove on the inside edges of the stiles and rails to hold the panels. Use a ¹⁄₈-in. straight bit in a table-mounted router. Mount stop blocks on the router table fence to prevent the cut from going through on the bottom rails (or they'll be visible in the tenon) **(PHOTO I)**.

**9.** Adjust the fence away from the router bit to widen the cut on each part to ³⁄₁₆ in. **(PHOTO J)**.

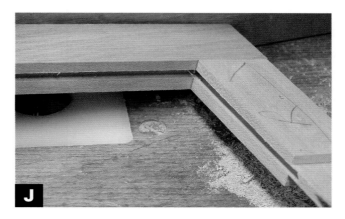

## Making the door panels

Resaw 4/4 stock to make the panels, using either a matching species or a contrasting wood. Resawing allows you to book-match the door panels. This method uses materials more efficiently, and the symmetry of book matching is especially pleasing to the eye.

**1.** Use the bandsaw with fence to make a cut down the middle of roughsawn 4/4 stock **(PHOTO K)**.

**RESAW 4/4 STOCK DOWN THE MIDDLE** to create ³⁄₈-in. stock for the front panels.

**FORM THE TONGUE** on three sides of the panel. First cut the tongue on the end by passing it between the blade and fence. Then cut the two long sides.

**FINISH THE TONGUE** by running it on edge along the tablesaw fence.

**2.** Plane the wood on both sides to a ⅜-in. thickness. Remove most of the material from the outside of the sawn halves so that the match on the inside remains as close as possible. Rip the stock to width on the tablesaw.

**3.** Set the tablesaw blade to a height of 3/16 in. to form the tongue around the edge of the panel. You could use a dado blade for this operation or you could first cut off the additional waste by setting the fence wide and then narrowing the distance for a final cut to form the 3/16-in. × 3/16-in. tongue. Use push sticks and featherboards to steady the work and keep your hands away from the blade. First make the cuts on the short grain edge (the bottom) **(PHOTO L)**. Then cut the tongue on the long edge **(PHOTO M)**.

WORK
**SMART**

When cutting joinery or routing edge treatments around a panel, cut the short grain sides first. If there's any tearout from cutting the short grain, the long grain cut will usually cut it off, leaving a clean edge.

**MARK A LINE** 3/16 in. from the first pencil line (toward the outside). This is your line for cutting the angled shape on the bandsaw.

**N**

**MARK THE SHAPE OF THE TOP STILE** on the top panel after assembling the frame to use as a template.

**4.** Assemble the stiles and rails of each door and set the panels underneath so you can trace the shape of the upper rail onto the panel **(PHOTO N)**.

**5.** Draw a line 3/16 in. away (in the direction of the top edge) from your traced line, so that you can use the bandsaw to cut the panel to its final shape **(PHOTO O)**. Sand the bandsawn edge smooth and then use the tablesaw to form the 3/16-in. × 3/16-in. tongue on the top edge of the panels, just as you did on the other edges.

# Shape and assemble the doors

**PRIOR TO ASSEMBLY OF THE DOORS,** sand those parts that will be difficult to sand later—namely, the inside edges of each part and the back side of each panel. Then to make the door parts look more finished, I add a small chamfered detail using the router table and a 45° router bit raised slightly above the router table. These small details add significantly to the viewer's engagement with the finished work. Make a practice cut on scrap stock to fine-tune the size of the chamfer.

**1.** Set the fence and rout the edge where the stiles intersect the rails **(PHOTO A)**.

**A**

**USE A 45° ROUTER BIT TO SHAPE THE EDGES** where the stiles and rails intersect. Hold the end of the workpiece tightly to the fence of the router table as you make the cut.

**SPREAD GLUE ON ALL THE SURFACES OF THE BRIDLE JOINTS**
before assembling the doors. Then use C-clamps to squeeze each joint, making
a secure and lasting glued joint.

**TRIM THE TENON END** where it protrudes beyond the inner door stiles.

**2.** Adjust the position of the fence to rout a matching profile on the edges of the door panels where they will intersect the stiles and rails. Use a 45° chamfer bit with a guide bearing to follow along the edge.

**3.** After final sanding, align the panel between the two stiles and spread glue on the tenons and push them into place. Use C-clamps to apply pressure to the outside of the joint to ensure a strong, durable glue joint **(PHOTO B)**. Allow the glue to dry completely.

**4.** Use the tablesaw to trim off the excess tenon material that protrudes beyond the inner door stiles **(PHOTO C)**.

# Make and install the hanger

**TO MAKE THE CABINET EASY TO HANG, ADD** a hanger strip to the back. The strip is beveled to mate with a similar strip that will be screwed to the wall. With this system the cabinet can be easily removed for cleaning or wall painting. In areas where there is a possibility of earthquakes, use an additional screw through the back of the cabinet into the wall or hanger strip after the cabinet is hung to make certain shaky ground won't cause the cabinet to jump free from its mount.

**1.** Make the hanger strips for the back of the cabinet and the wall at the same time, each ⅜ in. thick to match the space allowed at the back of the cabinet. On the tablesaw, cut a 35° angle on one edge of each strip **(PHOTO A)**. (See Step 4 on p. 11.)

**2.** Use woodworker's glue to secure the one strip to the back of the cabinet and then use screws when you are ready to level and secure the other to the wall **(PHOTO B)**.

**A**

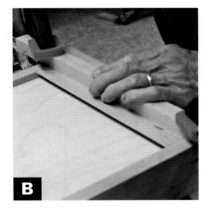

**B**

**BEVEL TWO STRIPS OF WOOD AT 35°. Glue one strip to the back. The mating strip hangs on the wall to hold the cabinet.**

# Rout the hinge mortises

**IF YOU'RE INSTALLING MORE THAN A PAIR** of hinges, you may find it easier to use a router and template rather than cutting the mortise by hand as shown on pp. 17–19. After many years of installing butt hinges by hand with a chisel, I discovered a simpler, more accurate, and faster router method. The process involves making a router template sized exactly to the dimensions of the hinge. The template can be made of thin plywood overlapped log cabin style at the corners.

**1.** Begin by ripping narrow strips of ¼-in. birch plywood **(PHOTO A)**.

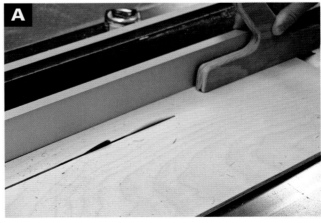

**A**

**RIP NARROW STRIPS OF ¼-IN. PLYWOOD. You'll use these to create a template for the router.**

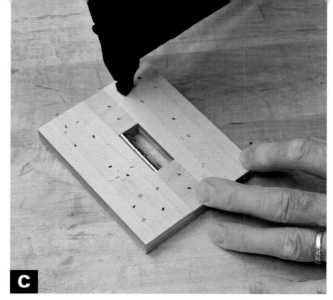

**BUILD THE SECOND LAYER,** using short brads to lock the plywood pieces in place.

**ARRANGE THE PLYWOOD STRIPS** around the hinge as shown. The pieces need to be long enough to overlap the side strips.

**A STRIP OF WOOD SECURED TO THE TEMPLATE** with countersunk screws enables you to clamp the template to the edge of the workpiece.

**2.** Cut the strips into short pieces equal to the dimensions of the closed hinge. For example, for a hinge with closed dimensions of $\frac{5}{8}$ in. × $1\frac{1}{2}$ in., you'll need two pieces $\frac{5}{8}$ in. long and two $1\frac{1}{2}$ in. long. Then to form the log cabin joints, you'll need pieces long enough to overlap the side strips. If the birch plywood is ripped into strips $1\frac{1}{2}$ in. wide, you will need two additional pieces $3\frac{5}{8}$ in. and two $4\frac{1}{2}$ in. to construct a log cabin assembly that surrounds the hinge **(PHOTO B)**. Enclose the hinge tightly with the plywood strips.

**3.** Build the second layer. As you fit the parts in place with corners overlapping, begin using short brads to join the layers together **(PHOTO C)**.

**4.** Screw a piece of plywood to the template so that the routing jig can be clamped to the workpiece **(PHOTO D)**. Position the mount so that the correct amount of hinge barrel will be exposed.

WORK
**SMART**

In order for a hinge to operate without binding, make sure that at least one-half of the hinge barrel is outside the mortise. In figuring the depth of the mortise, remember that you'll have the depth of one leaf in the door and the other in the cabinet.

**5.** To use the hinge template, clamp it in place and use a ½-in.-dia. dado cleanout bit to rout the mortise. A top-mounted bearing will follow the template and cut the shape of the hinge except for the corners, which will be left round. Leave the template in place to guide your chisel when squaring the corners **(PHOTO E)**.

**6.** To finish installing the hinges, follow the instructions on p. 19.

**SQUARE UP THE CORNERS** of the mortise with a corner chisel or straight chisel.

# Install the stop

**THE LAST STEP BEFORE APPLYING A FINISH** is installing a magnetic catch to each door.

**1.** Drill ⁵⁄₁₆-in. holes deep enough with a drill press for the magnetic catch **(PHOTO A)**. Too deep is better than too shallow, as once it is pushed in place, no amount of effort will get it out again.

**2.** Drill and countersink a mounting hole for a screw to attach the magnetic catches to the underside of the top of the cabinet **(PHOTO B)**.

**3.** Install the metal catch plates on the doors, then check the position of the doors in relation to the front edge of the cabinet while the magnetic catch unit is in place. Screw the block to the top of the cabinet.

**DRILL AND COUNTERSINK** a hole for the mounting screw. Install the metal catches on the doors, then drive the screw to attach the stop.

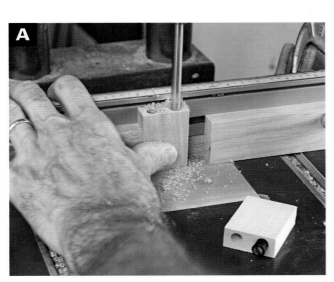

**DRILL FOR THE MAGNETIC CATCHES** with a drill press. Measure to make sure to drill deep enough.

# Finish

**FINISH THE** cabinet with Danish oil to bring out and protect the natural color of the wood.

**APPLYING AN OIL FINISH AND INSTALLING** the pulls are the last steps in the process. I chose Amerock pulls from the local hardware store to use on the doors. There are many choices, and your choice of pulls is one way of personalizing your cabinet. Other options include handmade pulls (several kinds are shown in this book), or you can come up with your own design. If using manufactured pulls, you will probably have to cut the screws shorter to use them with the ⅝-in.-thick cabinet doors.

**1.** Apply several coats of finish to all surfaces **(PHOTO A)**.

**2.** Install the pulls. If the screw is too long, use a bolt cutter to snip the screw off to the right length **(PHOTO B)**. You could choose to use a hack saw instead, but the bolt cutter presents an easy option.

**IF NECESSARY, USE BOLT CUTTERS** or a hack saw to cut the screws shorter. Then install the pulls on each door.

## DESIGN OPTIONS

**There are many ways to change the look of this cabinet. Use contrasting wood for the panels or try chip carving and milk paint for a colorful country look.**

**ONE EASY WAY TO ACHIEVE** a dramatically different look is to use book-matched panels of a dark wood species like walnut and build the cabinet of a lighter wood such as hickory or ash. The panels are made from a single piece of 4/4 rough stock bandsawn down the middle **(PHOTO A )**. Or use different colors of milk paint on the interior and other parts of the cabinet to create both texture and layers of color. A lighter color brightens the interior and makes it easier to see the contents **(PHOTO B )**.

**A**

**BOOK-MATCHED PANELS** are resawn from a single piece of rough stock.

**B**

**COLORFUL MILK PAINTS** add texture and a tough, durable surface. Mask off the interior as you paint to keep a smooth contrasting surface.

# Cherry Display Cabinet

**C**HERRY IS ONE of the most prized and beautiful of North American cabinet woods. Its working qualities are superb, and the deep reddish brown color that comes with age and exposure to light is much admired. But for the insides of a cabinet, it can seem too dark.

For this small wall-hung display cabinet, I applied a 1/8-in.-thick shopmade veneer to the inside surfaces to brighten the interior without having to resort to electric lights. The basswood shelves and equally light-colored Baltic-birch back also highlight the objects displayed inside.

The glass doors, angled in toward the center, make for an eyecatching design but also have a practical purpose by reducing glare and reflection. When you stand in front of the cabinet, you can clearly see the objects inside.

While the shape of the cabinet makes it appear complicated, all the cuts are at 5°. The sides are simply doweled to the top. For best results, work through the steps and take measurements from the completed assemblies, rather than cut all parts according to the cutlist.

For novice cabinetmakers, this design can be adapted to eliminate some of the more difficult steps, such as the angled cabinet sides. You can also substitute butt hinges for the knife hinges if you prefer.

# Cherry display cabinet

This design of this cabinet works to solve both practical and visual problems. The angled doors reduce glare in the glass and the lighter woods on the inside brighten the interior without artificial light.

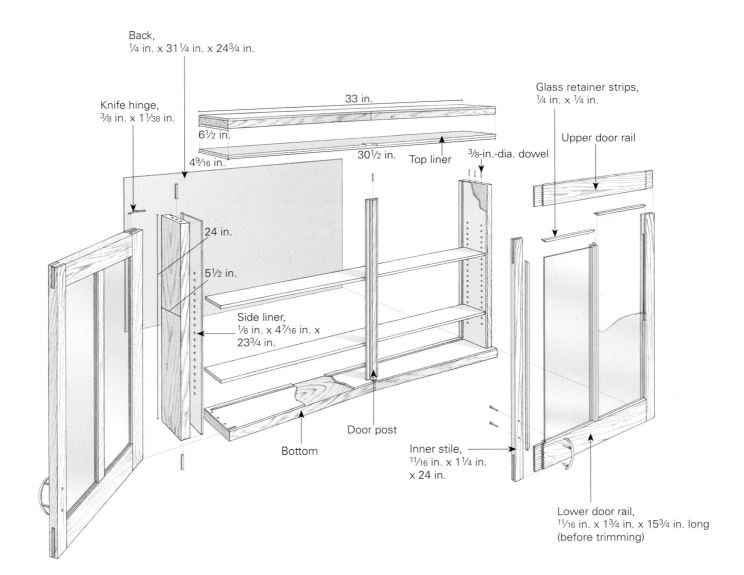

Back,
¼ in. x 31¼ in. x 24¾ in.

Knife hinge,
⅜ in. x 1¹/₃₈ in.

33 in.

6½ in.

4⁹/₁₆ in.

30½ in.

Top liner

⅜-in.-dia. dowel

Glass retainer strips,
¼ in. x ¼ in.

Upper door rail

24 in.

5½ in.

Side liner,
⅛ in. x 4⁷/₁₆ in. x 23¾ in.

Door post

Bottom

Inner stile,
¹¹/₁₆ in. x 1¼ in. x 24 in.

Lower door rail,
¹¹/₁₆ in. x 1¾ in. x 15¾ in. long
(before trimming)

# Top and bottom dimensions

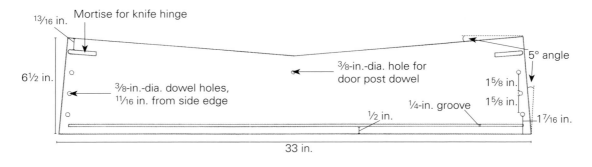

13/16 in.

Mortise for knife hinge

6½ in.

3/8-in.-dia. dowel holes, 11/16 in. from side edge

3/8-in.-dia. hole for door post dowel

5° angle

1 5/8 in.

1 5/8 in.

¼-in. groove

½ in.

1 7/16 in.

33 in.

## MATERIALS FOR CHERRY DISPLAY CABINET

| QUANTITY | PART | SIZE | NOTES |
|---|---|---|---|
| 2 | Top or bottom | 13/16 in. x 6½ in. x 33 in. | Cherry |
| 2 | Sides | 7/8 in. x 5½ in. x 24 in. | Cherry |
| 2 | Top or bottom liner | 1/8 in. x 4 9/16 in. 30½ in. | Basswood |
| 2 | Side liners | 1/8 in. x 4 7/16 in. x 23¾ in. | Basswood |
| 1 | Door post | 1 in. x 1¼ in. x 24 in. | Cherry |
| 2 | Outer door stiles | 11/16 in. x 1½ in. x 24 in. | Cherry |
| 2 | Inner door stiles | 11/16 in. x 1¼ in. x 24 in. | Cherry |
| 2 | Median door stiles | 11/16 in. x 7/8 in. x 22 3/16 in. | Cherry |
| 2 | Lower door rails | 11/16 in. x 1¾ in. x 15¾ in.* | Cherry |
| 2 | Upper door rails | 11/16 in. x 1½ in. x 15¾ in.* | Cherry |
| 2 | Shelves | 3/16 in. x 4 5/16 in. x 30¼ in. | Basswood |
| 1 | Back | ¼ in. x 31¼ in. x 24¾ in. | Baltic-birch plywood |
| 2 pr. | Knife hinges | 3/8 in. x 1¾ in. | Woodcraft #145289 |
| 8 | Glass retainer strips | ¼ in. x ¼ in. x 6 3/8 in. | Cherry |
| 8 | Glass retainer strips | ¼ in. x ¼ in. x 21¼ in. | Cherry |
| 48 | Steel brads | #19 ga. x ½ in. | |
| 16 | Shelf support pins | ¼ in. dia. x ¾ in. | Cut from hardwood dowel |
| 14 | Dowels | 3/8 in. dia. x 1½ | Commercial or cut from hardwood dowel |
| 2 | Magnetic catches | | |
| 4 | Glass panes | 1/8 in. x 6 5/8 in. x 21¼ in. | Double strength |

*Oversize in length to allow trimming flush to the door stiles.

# Make the top and bottom

**WHILE THE SHAPE OF THE CABINET SEEMS** complicated, it's actually quite simple. All of the angle cuts are 5°. Two different species of wood are required, cherry and basswood, and this cabinet can be easily simplified by making it all from a single, lighter colored species. Begin by planing and ripping the cherry stock to thickness and width.

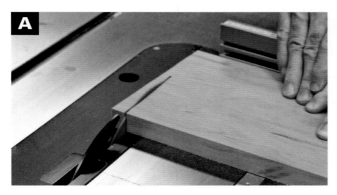

**MAKE THE CUTS** on each end of the top and bottom with the tablesaw miter gauge set to 5°.

**FIND THE CORRECT ANGLE** to cut the front of the top and bottom. Lay a square on each side and draw from the corners to center.

**1.** Use the tablesaw outfitted with a miter gauge set to cut a 5° angle at each end of the top and bottom **(PHOTO A)**.

**2.** Lay out the shape of the front of the cabinet on the top and bottom. Hold a carpenter's square tight to the end (or a square and straightedge) and draw a line from the corner toward the center. The lines will intersect at the center **(PHOTO B)**.

**3.** Double-check your layout lines to make sure that they intersect at the center. Measure across the back. Then use a square to form a line from the back to the front.

**4.** Use a bandsaw to make the cut. Cut on the outside of the pencil lines **(PHOTO C)**.

**CUT THE FRONT PROFILE** on the bandsaw. Stay just outside your line to allow smoothing after the cut.

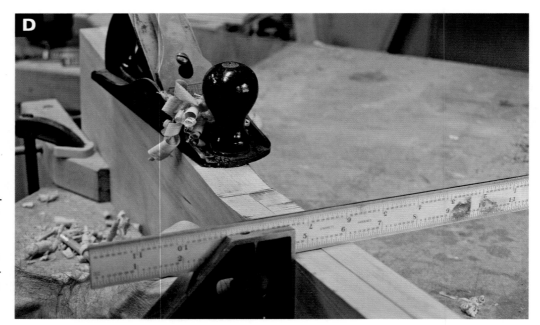

**CLAMP THE TOP** and bottom together and smooth the bandsawn edge with a handplane. Check frequently to make sure the edge remains square. Follow up with a random orbit sander but avoid rounding the point where the angles intersect.

**5.** Clamp the top and bottom together and use a plane to even the edges and remove the bandsaw marks. I use a #04 smoothing plane and check with a square to make sure I'm keeping my planed edges square to the surface of the stock **(PHOTO D)**.

**6.** Finish smoothing the edge with a random-orbit sander. Use a sanding block at the intersection of the angles to keep it crisp.

## Groove and dowel the top and bottom

**1.** Strike a gauge line on the inside surfaces of each end with a marking gauge. Adjust the pin to be $^{11}/_{16}$ in. from the gauge fence to locate the center of the dowel holes. This will locate the holes so they will be centered on the $^{7}/_{8}$-in.-thick sides and will position the sides $^{1}/_{4}$ in. from the edge **(PHOTO E)**. You will also use this mark to see where to end the groove for the back in the next step.

Routing the groove before drilling the dowel holes gives you a visual reference for locating the dowel holes.

**MAKE A MARKING GAUGE LINE** $^{11}/_{16}$ **in. from the end of the top and bottom to locate the center of the dowel holes.**

**2.** Rout the groove on the inside surfaces of the top and bottom using a plunge router outfitted with a ¼-in. straight bit and edge guide. You'll cut the ⅜-in.-deep groove ½ in. from the back edge **(PHOTO F)**. While a shallower groove would have been sufficient for the ¼-in. Baltic-birch plywood back in place, I decided to use a ⅜-in. deep groove so that the panel could be glued in place and provide greater structural strength to the cabinet.

**3.** Mark the locations for the dowel holes. The first hole should be 1¾ in. from the front edge, allowing for the ¼-in. reveal as well as ¾ in. for the thickness of the door (including a slight clearance between the doors and sides). Mark off the next hole 1⅝ in. from the first, and space the third hole 1⅝ in. from the second. Mark the intersections between the marking gauge line and the measured dowel locations using an awl to provide a positive location for the drill bit.

**4.** Use the drill press to drill the dowel holes to a depth of ⅝ in. Set the depth carefully so that the drill bit does not go through. Use a brad point bit to allow for the easiest and most accurate alignment of your drill bit with the marks **(PHOTO G)**.

**ROUT THE GROOVE FOR THE BACK** on the inside surfaces of the top and bottom with a plunge router and edge guide.

**DRILL THE DOWEL HOLES ON THE DRILL PRESS.** Using a brad point bit makes it easier to center the bit on your marks. Also drill the holes for the door post.

**5.** Use the drill press to drill the dowel holes to secure the door post. This hole should be exactly centered between the ends of the top and bottom and 4⁵⁄₁₆ in. from the back edge. This will maintain the ¼-in. setback from the front edge to the surface of the doors.

WORK
**SMART**

Some drills are now equipped with laser guides, but they are only as accurate as your attention in setting them up and the care with which you have laid out your marks.

# Make the sides and door post

**THE SIDES OF THE CABINET ARE CUT AT 90°** on the front edge and at 85° at the back because the sides are set at a 5° angle to the back. For that reason, you'll need to cut an angled groove for the back. Plane the stock for the sides to ⅞ in. thick, joint one edge on the jointer, and then cut the other at 85° on the tablesaw. For the door post, plane and rip cherry stock to a dimension of 1 in. × 1½ in.

**B**

**FORM THE DOOR STOPS** in the post by making 5° cuts into it on both sides. Then lower the blade, put the inside face against the blade, and make a meeting cut.

**A**

**TILT THE BLADE AT 85° TO CUT THE GROOVES** on the sides for the back panel. Move the fence away from the blade to widen the groove to ¼ in.

**1.** Cut the groove for the back on the tablesaw. Set the blade height at ⅜ in. and set the fence so that ½ in. remains between the outside edge of the groove and the back of the side. Move the fence ⅛ in. closer to the blade for the second pass, widening the cut to fit the ¼-in. plywood back **(PHOTO A)**.

**2.** With the blade at the same angle used to cut grooves for the back to fit, set the blade height at ¾ in. above the surface of the saw. I mark on the end of the stock so that I can observe that the blade cuts ⅞ in. from the inside edge of the stock.

In other words, the saw cut is ⅞ in. from the edge of the stock. Make a cut with one edge against the fence and then turn the stock end for end to cut the other **(PHOTO B)**.

**3.** Adjust the fence and lower the blade so that it intersects the previous cuts with the post's inside edge against the fence. Cut the sides to length using the sled on the tablesaw to ensure accuracy.

**4.** Use a doweling jig to drill into the ends of the sides. Drill to a depth of 1⅛ in. **(PHOTO C)**.

**C**

**USE A DOWELING JIG** to drill the dowel holes in the ends of the cabinet sides. Use a depth stop to limit the depth of the hole.

**5.** Use the doweling jig to drill into the center of the end of the door post. Align the jig so that the hole will be perfectly in the center of the post end **(PHOTO D)**.

**WORK SMART**

When using a doweling jig for the first time, make test holes in scrap stock to make certain that the markings of the jig are in perfect alignment. This is especially critical when only one dowel is being used at each end of the stock.

**D**

**DRILL DOWEL HOLES** at each end of the door post. Very careful alignment is critical so that the door stop is perfectly centered and vertical in the finished cabinet.

# Build the doors

**NOW THAT THE SIDES, TOP, BOTTOM, AND** door post are doweled, do a trial assembly and double-check the dimensions for the doors. If you've followed the cutlist exactly, the opening top to bottom and from the inside edge of the door post should measure 24 in. × 15½ in. If not, adjust the sizes of the doors by lengthening or shortening parts. Note that I leave the rails slightly longer so that they can be trimmed flush to the stiles after

assembly. Also, to simplify the construction process I cut all tenons to the same length and trim them accordingly. I planned for double-strength glass in cutting the depth of the rabbets, so they are cut ⅜ in. deep, ⅛ in. for the glass, and ¼ in. for the strip to hold the glass in place (see the drawing on p. 64).

**1.** After planing and ripping the door stock to size, use a sled on the tablesaw with a stop block to control the exact length. Keep small pieces of cut-off stock to help in setting up the following operations. It is best to make your mistakes in scrap wood, rather than in your finest cherry.

**2.** Use a tenoning jig on the tablesaw to cut the slots forming the bridle joints in the door stiles. Make the cuts at the top of the stiles with the blade height set at 1¼ in. For the bottom slots, raise the blade to 1½ in. You'll make two cuts to create the ¼-in.-wide slot. Keep the inside face of the stock against the jig. Make your first ⅛-in. cut at ¼ in., then adjust the jig to widen the cut to the ¼ in. (**PHOTO A** on p. 62).

## DOOR PROPORTIONS

I often use wider stock to form the bottom rails of small cabinet doors. This compensates for the effect of seeing the bottom rails at a distance. If the rails, top and bottom, were the same size, the lower one would appear smaller, because it's farther from the eye. So in this cabinet, the upper rails are 1½ in. wide, and the lower rails are 1¾ in. wide. You will also notice that I've designed the door stiles to be narrower at the center, which allows more of the cabinet interior to be visible.

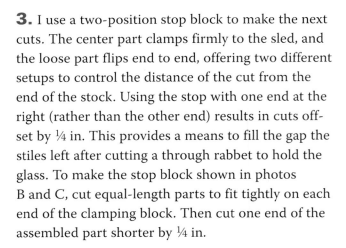

**3.** I use a two-position stop block to make the next cuts. The center part clamps firmly to the sled, and the loose part flips end to end, offering two different setups to control the distance of the cut from the end of the stock. Using the stop with one end at the right (rather than the other end) results in cuts offset by ¼ in. This provides a means to fill the gap the stiles left after cutting a through rabbet to hold the glass. To make the stop block shown in photos B and C, cut equal-length parts to fit tightly on each end of the clamping block. Then cut one end of the assembled part shorter by ¼ in.

**4.** With the stop block set to cut the shoulder at $1^{9/16}$ in. and the outside face (the front) of the rail down, make a ³⁄₁₆-in.-deep cut (**PHOTO B**).

**5.** Without moving the clamp securing the block to the sled, turn the stop block over to use the side that positions the $1^{5/16}$-in. cut. Raise the blade to make a ¼-in.-deep cut and cut with the back of the rail down (**PHOTO C**).

**6.** Cut the tenon cheeks using a tenoning jig. Make the first cuts with the blade height set at $1^{5/16}$ in. and with the back side of the rail against the body of the jig (**PHOTO D**). Adjust the jig to cut the opposite cheek and raise the blade height to $1^{9/16}$ in.

**CUT THE SLOTS AT THE ENDS** of the door stiles on the tablesaw with a tenoning jig. I make a cut on each piece and then adjust the jig to widen the cut to ¼ in.

**MAKE A ³⁄₁₆-IN.-DEEP CUT** in each end of the door rails with the outside face down on the surface of the sled.

**REVERSE THE STOP BLOCK** so that the cut is now ¼ in. closer to the end of the rail. This distance is $1^{5/16}$ in. from the end of the rail. Raise the blade to make a ¼-in.-deep cut.

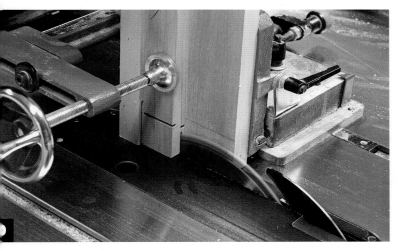

FINISH FORMING THE TENONS by using the tenoning jig on the tablesaw. All these cuts are made with the back of the rail facing the jig.

**7.** Cut the rabbets at the inside face of the door stiles, rails, and median stiles. For the first cut, the back of the part is flat on the tablesaw with the blade height at ⅜ in. and the fence set to make a ¼-in.-wide cut. To complete the rabbet, lower the blade height to ¼ in. and set the fence to a ⅜-in.-wide cut. This time you'll cut with the part on edge and the back of the stile against the fence **(PHOTO E)**.

**8.** Now that the rabbets are cut, you can complete the tenons on the tablesaw using the crosscut sled. The first cut is made with the stock standing on end and with a stop block setting the distance of the cut ¼ in. from the edge **(PHOTO F)**.

**9.** Then use the sliding stop block to finish the cut. I set the blade height at ¼ in. and the distance between the stop block so that the blade aligns with the longer shoulder of the tenon. Use the sliding stop tight to your left to locate the position of the cut. Then slide it to your right to get it out of the way as the piece is cut **(PHOTO G)**.

CUT THE RABBETS. The first cut is made with the back side face down on the tablesaw. Adjust the blade height and the position of the fence to finish the rabbets with the back side against the fence.

TRIM THE TENONS to width. Clamp the rail to the fence of the crosscut sled.

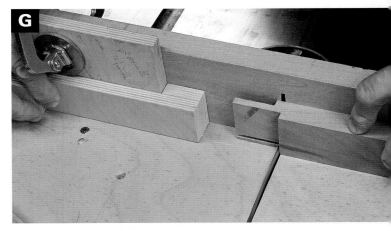

FINISH THE CUT with the piece on edge. Align the workpiece using a sliding stop block.

**H**

**TO CUT THE MEDIAN-STILE TENONS**
use the same process as for tenoning the rails.
Make offset shoulder cuts with the crosscut
sled. Use the tenoning jig to cut the cheeks.
Then cut rabbets on both sides of the rear face.

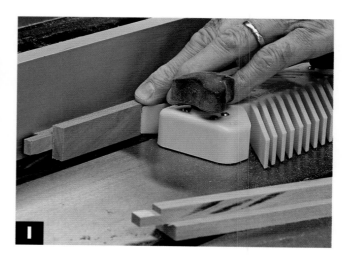

**I**

**10.** Use the same steps that you used for the rails
for cutting the tenons at the ends of the door post.
Begin by making the offset shoulder cuts and complete the tenons on the tenoning jig **(PHOTO H)**.
Then cut ¼-in.-wide × ⅜-in. rabbets on each side
of the back face for the glass and retainer strips
**(PHOTO I)**.

**11.** Use the drill press and a ¼-in. drill bit to define
the mortises for the median stiles. I drill two holes
¼ in. apart against the edge of the rabbet and just
over ½ in. deep. Use a chisel to remove the waste
between the drilled holes **(PHOTO J)**.

## Door detail

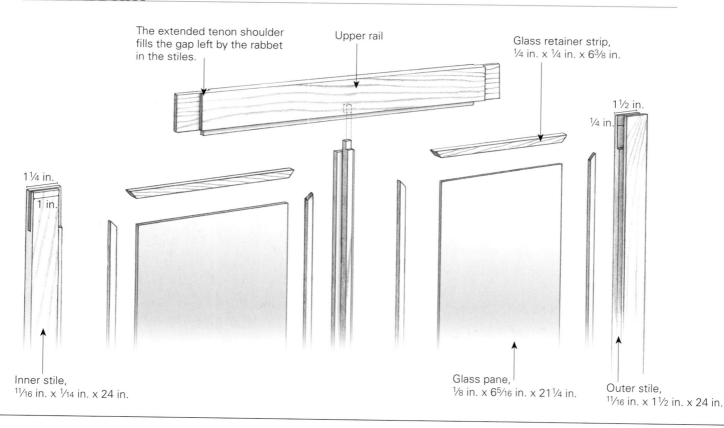

The extended tenon shoulder
fills the gap left by the rabbet
in the stiles.

Upper rail

Glass retainer strip,
¼ in. x ¼ in. x 6⅜ in.

1½ in.

¼ in.

1¼ in.

1 in.

Inner stile,
¹¹⁄₁₆ in. x ¹⁄₁₄ in. x 24 in.

Glass pane,
⅛ in. x 6⁵⁄₁₆ in. x 21¼ in.

Outer stile,
¹¹⁄₁₆ in. x 1½ in. x 24 in.

USE A ¼-IN. DRILL BIT IN THE DRILL PRESS to cut the mortises in the rails for the median stiles. Chisel out the waste between holes. The mortises are longer than required but will be covered with the retainer strips.

**12.** Glue the door joints, then put the assembled door frames up on level blocks to make sure the door isn't twisted. Use C-clamps to tighten the slots in the stiles onto the tenoned rails.

**13.** After the glue has fully dried, remove the clamps and use the miter gauge on the tablesaw to trim the rails flush to the stiles. Try the door in the opening and remove enough from the top and bottom for a ¹⁄₁₆-in. clearance at each end. Use a sanding block to smooth the edges.

## Cut the knife-hinge mortises in the top and bottom

Knife hinges show very little on the outside of the cabinet, providing a clean, modern look. Many people use laborious hand techniques to install them. I prefer to use a router to do most of the work, thereby eliminating most of the hand chiseling. Use a plunge router to cut the mortises for the hinges in the top and bottom. After the cabinet has been assembled and you've trimmed the doors to final height and width, use the router table to cut the mortises in the doors.

**1.** To set up for routing the hinge mortises in the top and bottom, cut a block of wood to use as a setup guide. Measure the width of the router base, add the length the bit must travel, and subtract the diameter of the bit. My router base measures 6¼ in. The hinges measure 1¾ in. and the diameter of the router bit is ³⁄₈ in. (base + travel distance − bit diameter = 7⁵⁄₈ in.) Your router base may be different, so be sure to measure it carefully. Mark a line at the very center of the guide block.

**2.** Mark the centerline of the hinge on the front edge of the top and bottom for both doors. Set the hinge so that it will protrude ¹⁄₈ in. beyond the edge of the door. (The alignment mark will be 1 in. from each end of the top and bottom parts.)

**3.** Align the guide block with the mark on the edge of the top or bottom and use it to locate stop blocks to control the travel of the router. Be sure to clamp the stop blocks firmly in place. While routing one part, I use its opposite end as a foundation for the outside stop block **(PHOTO K)**.

TO ROUT MORTISES FOR THE KNIFE HINGES, use a spacer to guide the positioning of stop blocks to control router travel. Mark the center of the guide spacer and align that mark with the center of the hinge location.

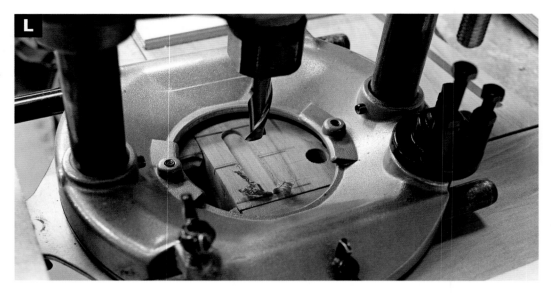

**SET THE FENCE** on the plunge router to position the hinge mortise from the edge. The ³⁄₈-in. router bit cuts a groove exactly matching the width of the ³⁄₈-in. knife hinges. Stop blocks control the router travel. Set the depth of cut to equal the thickness of the hinge leaf.

**USE A ³⁄₈-IN. CHISEL TO SQUARE UP ONE END** of the mortise to match the profile of the hinge.

**4.** Rout the hinge mortise. Set the fence on the router so that the bit will cut the correct distance of the hinge from the edge, and set the depth of the cut so that one leaf of the hinge comes out flush with the surface of the wood **(PHOTO L)**.

**5.** Use a ³⁄₈-in. chisel to square the end for each hinge mortise, leaving the outside ends round to match the shape of the hinge **(PHOTO M)**.

# Make the shelves and liners

**RESAW BASSWOOD STOCK** on the tablesaw. Use a push stick to keep your fingers away from the blade.

**RESAW BASSWOOD ON THE TABLESAW TO** prepare stock to make the shelves and inside liners. Raise the blade to a height equal to just over half the width of the stock, make a cut on one edge, then flip the board around to cut from the other side. You can also use the bandsaw to resaw the stock. For the shelves and the inside liners you'll need a total of three pieces of 4/4 basswood stock, 31 in. long.

**1.** Cut two ⁵⁄₁₆-in.-thick pieces from 5-in.-wide 4/4 stock on the tablesaw. The remaining thin piece can be used for the inner liner of the top, bottom, or sides **(PHOTO A)**.

**2.** Plane the material for the shelves to a thickness of ³⁄₁₆ in. and then plane the remaining material to a thickness of ⅛ in.

**3.** Joint one edge of the stock and cut it to a uniform width of 4¾ in.

**4.** Mark the angled cuts at the front of the shelves and top and bottom liners. Make the cut on the bandsaw, staying just outside the lines (see p. 57).

**5.** Clamp the shelves and top and bottom liners to the top or bottom and use it as a routing template. Position the part to be routed 1¾ in. from the back edge of your template. Use a laminate trimmer and piloted cutter to trim them flush **(PHOTO B)**. Guide the router from the right to the left to avoid tearout.

**6.** Cut the top and bottom liners to length with a 5° angle at each end. To determine the exact location of the cut, measure an equal distance to each end from the center. Double-check the clearance at each end for the sides (approximately 1 in. from the ends of the top and the bottom).

**WORK SMART**

When routing thin multiples such as the top and bottom liner and shelves for this project, you can gang them by clamping two or three together and routing them at the same time.

# Install the liners

**1.** Before gluing the basswood liners in place, sand the inside surfaces of the top, bottom, and sides.

**2.** Rout the edges of the top and bottom using a 45° chamfering bit. Also rout the edges of the liner stock with a 1/16-in. roundover bit and double-check the dimensions.

**3.** Cut the side liner parts to the same length or very slightly shorter than the sides. Cutting them to exact length can be done more accurately after they are glued in place. Short scraps of Baltic-birch plywood inserted in the grooves will help with the positioning of the parts before clamping. Get those ready before you start. Spread glue on the inside surfaces of the basswood liner parts. I use common Elmer's® Glue-All®, which is thin, spreads easily, and gives a long open time. Do just one part at a time, and then its opposite side so the pieces can be clamped face to face.

**4.** Prepare to glue the liners to the top and bottom by tacking retainers in place. Note in **PHOTO C** how to place plywood scraps in the grooves and the strips tacked at the ends to keep the liner stock from moving as clamping pressure is applied.

**5.** Place the top and bottom and the two sides face to face to clamp them together as pairs to distribute clamping pressure as the liners are glued in place **(PHOTO D)**.

**PLACE SCRAPS OF PLYWOOD IN THE GROOVE and at either end of the top and bottom to prevent the glued liner from shifting while you apply the clamps.**

**GLUE LIKE PARTS AS PAIRS to distribute the clamping pressure evenly. Use plenty of clamps.**

# Prepare for assembly

**BEFORE ASSEMBLY, YOU'LL NEED TO FIT THE** door post. You'll need to drill holes in the sides and in the door post to hold the shelf support pins. Without the supports at the center, the shelves would need to be thicker to be equally strong.

**1.** Use the front divider as a guide to chisel out the top and bottom lining for it to fit. I insert a dowel into the top or bottom and into the end of the door post and use the post as my guide for marking where to remove material. Use a sharp pencil or marking knife **(PHOTO A)**.

**2.** Use a chisel to remove the stock necessary for the front divider to fit between the top and the bottom.

**3.** Set the height of the tablesaw blade at $\frac{1}{8}$ in. to trim the inner side linings to final length. Set the fence so that the space to the blade is $\frac{7}{8}$ in., equal to the thickness of the cabinet sides **(PHOTO B)**.

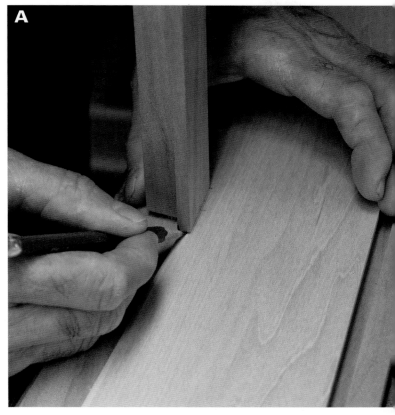

**INSERT A DOWEL** into the door post. Trace the position onto the top and bottom liners with a sharp pencil or marking knife. Accuracy is important. Then remove the waste with a straight chisel.

**TRIM THE ENDS** of the sides using a tablesaw with the blade raised $\frac{1}{8}$ in. high and with the space between the fence and blade equal to the thickness of the cherry sides ($\frac{7}{8}$ in.).

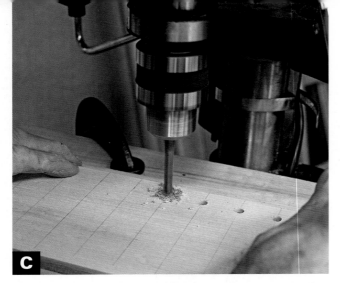

**DRILL THE SHELF SUPPORT HOLES** to a depth of ⅝ in. I use a fence on the drill press table and pencil lines to position the holes. The holes are spaced 1 in. apart.

**4.** Mark the locations for the shelf support holes in the sides and the front divider. The holes are ⅞ in. from the edges of the sides. Be sure to measure from the very end of the cabinet sides and divider and not from the end of the side liners, so that the holes in the front piece and ends will be evenly placed.

**5.** Use the drill press to drill holes for shelf supports. I use a fence clamped to the table of the drill press to control the distance from the edge, and then use the pencil marks to indicate the distance from the bottom of the cabinet sides **(PHOTO C)**.

# Assemble the cabinet

**SAND ALL THE INTERIOR PARTS BEFORE** assembly. If you haven't done a trial assembly, make sure to do it now in case any dowels are misaligned. Cut the back panel from Baltic-birch plywood and sand it thoroughly. I sand the edges smooth so they fit more easily into the grooves.

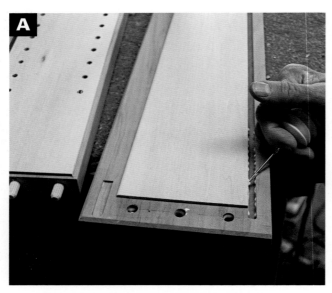

A

**GLUE AT THE ENDS OF THE GROOVES** for the back panel adds structural rigidity to the cabinet.

**1.** Spread glue in the dowel holes. Put a bit of glue into each end of the grooves. This will make the back panel a structural part of the cabinet and give it more rigidity than dowels alone **(PHOTO A)**.

**2.** Push the dowels in place and clamp the cabinet. Putting the cabinet doors in place helps you see if the cabinet is going together absolutely square to the doors **(PHOTO B)**.

**3.** Cut and fit a hanger for the back. I used basswood ripsawn at a 35° angle and secured it with glue at the back of the cabinet (see p. 49). Angle the ends at 5° to conform to the back edge of the sides.

WORK
**SMART**

Use blocks of wood or pads when clamping the cabinet to avoid marring the surfaces.

USE PIPE OR BAR CLAMPS to pull the top and bottom tightly to the sides and back. I use wood pads to keep the steel jaws from marring the cherry.

# Complete the doors

**THERE ARE TWO MORE STEPS TO COMPLETE** the doors: routing the profile and installing the knife hinges. The router table offers a secure and accurate option for routing the hinge mortises in the door. I use a story stick to set up the router table, fence, and stops.

**1.** Rout the inside of the door frames using a piloted chamfering bit in a hand-held router. Finish up the cuts on the corners using a straight chisel **(PHOTO A)**.

USE A CHAMFERING BIT in the router to rout the inside edges of the doors and then use a straight chisel to clean up the cut in the corners where the router bit bearing prevents a finished cut.

First, measure the distance from the edge of the cabinet sides to the location of the hinge mortises in the cabinet to determine the best distance to locate the fence from the $\frac{3}{8}$-in. straight-cut router bit. The distance from the fence to the router bit should be $\frac{1}{32}$ in. closer to the fence than the distance from the cabinet side to the routed mortises in the top and bottom. This is to provide $\frac{1}{32}$-in. clearance between the doors and the cabinet sides. Too tight a fit invites binding. I prefer to make two passes to make certain the fit is just right. The story stick makes it easy to come back and make a second, deeper cut if necessary.

**2.** Make a story stick using thin stock. Use $\frac{1}{8}$-in. Baltic-birch plywood scrap or basswood left over from the liners. Set a stop block so that it measures $1\frac{5}{8}$ in. from it to the opposite side of the router bit. Mark the story stick with a line $1\frac{5}{8}$ in. from the end and use it as a test piece. Rout the story stick and lay it over the mortise in the cabinet. You'll be able to see the exact clearance between the door and cabinet sides when the hinges are installed. If you're not satisfied with the amount of clearance, you can change the location of the fence either to make things tighter or to increase the distance between the door and cabinet sides **(PHOTO B)**.

**A STORY STICK** helps set up the distance of the stop block to the far side of the router bit. This will enable exact routing of the bottom of the right door and the top of the left. The back side of the door is against the fence.

**REVERSE THE SETUP TO** rout the remaining mortises.

**D**

EXCEPT FOR SOME CLEANUP WORK with a ⅜-in. chisel, the mortise is complete.

**E**

MOUNT A BRAD IN THE DRILL PRESS to use as a bit to drill pilot holes in the glass retainer strips.

**F**

PROTECT THE GLASS WITH CARDBOARD as you drive in the brads. A piece of wood on the opposite side of the hammer provides firm backing as the nails are driven into the median stile.

**3.** Set the bit height so that one leaf of the hinge will fit flush to the surface of the door. When you are certain of your setup, rout the hinge mortises on the top of the right door and the bottom of the left with the inside of the door against the fence. Hold the door tight to the fence and move it toward the stop block and back.

**4.** To rout the opposite hinge, flip the story stick end for end, and place the stop block on the opposite side, tight against the router bit **(PHOTO C)**.

**5.** Fit the hinges into the routed recess, making any necessary adjustments with a ⅜-in. straight chisel **(PHOTO D)**.

**6.** Make the glass retainer strips from ¼-in.-sq. stock and miter them at the ends to fit the insides of the doors. Cut all the long pieces first and then cut the 8 shorter pieces from what's left.

**7.** Drill pilot holes in the retainer strips using a ½-in. × #19-gauge brad as a bit in the drill press **(PHOTO E)**.

**8.** Use a cushion of cardboard between the hammer and glass to prevent scratching. A block of wood between the median stile and the other side of the door provides support. If you see a nail start to bend in the slightest, stop and replace it before it bends too much to drive it to full depth **(PHOTO F)**.

WORK
**SMART**

You can use a nail gun for this task, but you run the risk of broken glass if a nail goes astray, and it is easier to remove hammered-in-place brads than pneumatic ones in the event that glass needs to be replaced.

# Mission
# Display Cabinet

I **LIVE IN A SMALL** tourist town with a vibrant historic downtown filled with small shops and galleries. Eureka Springs, Arkansas, is also the home of innumerable artists and many patrons of the arts. As a local woodworker, I have made many small cabinets to house small collections of art objects or to be used for selling artists' work at craft shows. Some of my small cabinets are used in our local history museum to display artifacts of town history.

This small cabinet is inspired by the work of Gustav Stickley from the Arts and Crafts era. The width of the cabinet at the base gives it a secure feel. The cabinet sides are joined to the top and bottom through the use of wedged tenons, a technique made popular during the Arts and Crafts movement. Glass panels on both the front and the back help bring ambient light into the cabinet, eliminating the need for in-cabinet lighting.

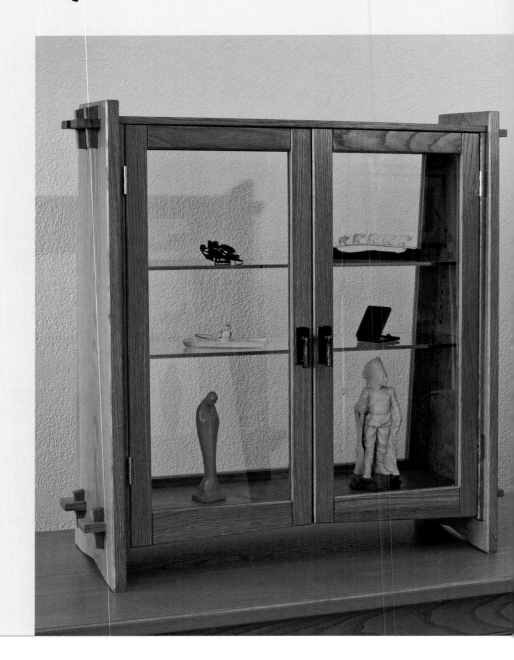

# Mission display cabinet

Wedged, through tenons are a signature of Stickley furniture of the Arts and Crafts era. This display cabinet uses biscuits to simplify the alignment of the angled doors and front panel during assembly.

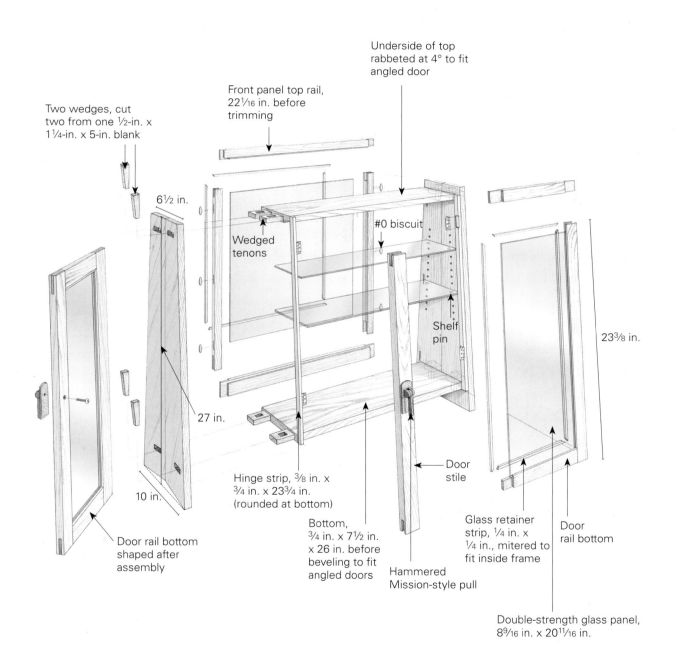

Two wedges, cut two from one 1/2-in. x 1 1/4-in. x 5-in. blank

Front panel top rail, 22 1/16 in. before trimming

Underside of top rabbeted at 4° to fit angled door

6 1/2 in.

Wedged tenons

#0 biscuit

Shelf pin

23 3/8 in.

27 in.

10 in.

Door rail bottom shaped after assembly

Hinge strip, 3/8 in. x 3/4 in. x 23 3/4 in. (rounded at bottom)

Bottom, 3/4 in. x 7 1/2 in. x 26 in. before beveling to fit angled doors

Door stile

Hammered Mission-style pull

Glass retainer strip, 1/4 in. x 1/4 in., mitered to fit inside frame

Door rail bottom

Double-strength glass panel, 8 9/16 in. x 20 11/16 in.

## MATERIALS FOR MISSION DISPLAY CABINET

| QUANTITY | PART | SIZE | NOTES |
|---|---|---|---|
| 2 | Sides | ¾ in. × 10 in. × 27 in. | White oak |
| 1 | Top | ¾ in. × 6 in. × 26 in. | White oak |
| 1 | Bottom | ¾ in. × 7½ in. × 26 in.* | White oak |
| 4 | Door stiles | ¹¹⁄₁₆ in. × 1¼ in. × 23⅜ in. | White oak |
| 2 | Top door rails | ¹¹⁄₁₆ in. × 1¼ in. × 10¹¹⁄₁₆ in.† | White oak |
| 2 | Bottom door rails | ¹¹⁄₁₆ in. × 2 in. × 10¹¹⁄₁₆ in. | White oak |
| 2 | Hinge strips | ¾ in. × ⅜ in. 23¾ in.‡ | White oak |
| 2 | Front panel stiles | ¹¹⁄₁₆ in. × 1¼ in. × 23⅜ in. | White oak |
| 1 | Front panel rail top | ¹¹⁄₁₆ in. × 1¼ in. × 22¹⁄₁₆ in. | White oak |
| 1 | Front panel rail bottom | ¹¹⁄₁₆ in. × 2 in. × 22¹⁄₁₆ in. | White oak |
| 8 | Wedges | ½ in. thick × 5 in. long (tapered from ¾ in. to ⅜ in.)§ | White oak |
| 2 pr. | Narrow brass hinges | ⅞ in. × 1½ in. | Ace Hardware stock #5299755 |
| 4 | Glass retainer strips | ¼ in. × ¼ in. × 8⅝ in. | White oak |
| 6 | Glass retainer strips | ¼ in. × ¼ in. × 20⅝ in. | White oak |
| 2 | Glass retainer strips | ¼ in. × ¼ in. × 20 in. | White oak |
| 12 | Biscuits | #0 | |
| 2 | Mission-style pulls | ⅞ in. × 2⅜ in. | Hammered brass, Rockler™ stock #26815 |
| 32 | Wire brads | ½ in. × 19 gauge | Steel |
| 2 | Glass door panels | 8⁹⁄₁₆ in. × 20¹¹⁄₁₆ in. | Double-strength glass |
| 1 | Glass front panel | 19¹⁵⁄₁₆ in. × 20¹¹⁄₁₆ in. | Double-strength glass |
| 1 | Glass shelf upper | ¼ in. × 5 in. × 21⅞ in. | Edges polished |
| 1 | Glass shelf lower | ¼ in. × 5¾ in. × 21⅞ in. | Edges polished |
| 8 | Shelf support pins | ¼ in. dia. × ¾ in. | Cut from wooden dowels |

*Rough width; trim to final width after cutting the tenons. †All rails are long to allow for trimming tenons flush to the sides after assembly. ‡Rounded at the bottom; they provide ¹⁄₁₆-in. clearance at the back of the doors to prevent hinge binding. §Cut two from one ½-in. × 1¼-in. × 5-in. blank; trim to final length and angle after gluing and assembly.

# Make the sides

**PLANE YOUR MATERIALS FOR THE CABINET** top, bottom, and sides to a thickness of ¾ in. Pass one edge of each piece across the jointer to make sure it is straight and square. If you don't have material wide enough to yield boards for the sides of 10-in. final width, glue up a panel from narrower stock before planing to final thickness. Crosscut the sides to the finished length of 27 in.

**1.** Lay out the mortises before the sides are tapered. Square stock of equal length end to end makes it easier to check the position of the joinery accurately. Mark the locations of the mortises in the sides **(PHOTO A)**, referring to the drawing below.

**2.** Use a ½-in. mortising bit in a hollow-chisel mortiser to cut the mortises. (If you don't have a

**A**

**CAREFULLY LAY OUT THE MORTISES** in the sides. I shade the area to be removed so I can double-check the setup on the mortiser.

mortiser, you can cut the mortises by hand or use a drill press or plunge router to remove most of the waste and then square the holes with a chisel.) Set

## Carcase detail

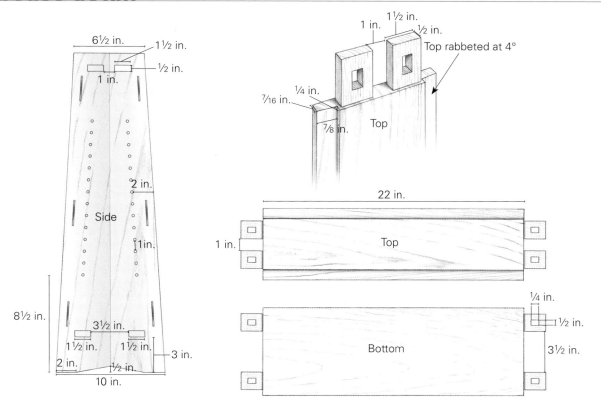

**CUT FROM THE OUTSIDE** toward the inside. Make the outside cuts of each mortise first, and then remove the remaining waste at the center.

B

**WORK SMART**

When cutting a mortise at the end of a board, use an accessory stand to support the other end.

C

**JOINT THE EDGES** to straighten the bandsaw cuts on each side with a jointer.

D

**MEASURE ½ IN.** from the center at the bottom and 2 in. from each side. Cut the small triangle of waste with a bandsaw.

up the fence on the mortiser to control the distance of the mortise from the bottom edge and use a stop block to control the distance from the edge. Use a backer board under the board you are mortising to minimize tearout. Cut the outside edges of the mortise first and then cut out the waste at the center. This will ensure that the mortising bit doesn't wander and that the mortise will be at the same dimension on both sides of the stock **(PHOTO B)**.

**3.** Lay out the angle of the sides. Make a pencil mark 1¾ in. along the top from each top corner and then use a straightedge and pencil to mark from each bottom corner to the marks at the top to form the tapering sides as shown in the drawing on p. 77. Use the bandsaw to cut along the lines on the waste side.

**4.** Run the edge of the sides on the jointer to make the final cuts down to the lines. This cleans up the bandsaw marks and ensures a straight edge on the front and back of each side **(PHOTO C)**.

**5.** Measure ½ in. up from the bottom edge at the center of each side and make marks from 2 in. in from each side edge. Connect the marks. Use a bandsaw to remove the waste **(PHOTO D)**. Then use a sanding block to remove the bandsaw marks.

# Make the top and bottom

**AFTER CUTTING THE PARTS TO LENGTH AND**
a slightly oversize width (see p. 76), begin by cutting the shoulders of the tenons. Use a crosscut sled on the tablesaw with a stop block to ensure that the tenon shoulders will be the same distance from each end. Cutting a ½-in.-thick tenon from ¾-in. stock requires that ⅛ in. be cut from each side.

**1.** Cut the shoulders on the crosscut sled. Set the blade height at ⅛ in. and set the stop block so that the resulting tenon will be 2 in. long. Make the same cut on each end and each side of the top and bottom parts **(PHOTO A)**.

**2.** Set the part on end to make the vertical cuts to the shoulder lines. Use clamps to secure the stock in place for each cut. This will keep your hands clear from the area to be cut. Adjust the height of the blade to reach the cut line left in the preceding operation and use the stop block to position the workpiece for each cut. Be careful that the blade cut is not too high. You can use a chisel to trim

**BEGIN FORMING THE TENONS** on the top and bottom using the tablesaw sled and stop block to control the position of the cut. Raise the blade ⅛ in. above the surface of the sled for this cut.

a cut that's shy, but a cut too high can't be fixed. This requires a number of steps. To cut the space between the tenons, set the stop block to define the tenons and then gradually move the stock away from the stop block for successive cuts until the full space between the tenons is removed **(PHOTO B)**.

**USE THE TABLESAW SLED** and stop block to cut the tenons in each end of the top and bottom. Use clamps to secure the workpiece to the sled. Cut the space between the tenons by making repetitive adjacent cuts until all the waste is removed.

## Tenon detail

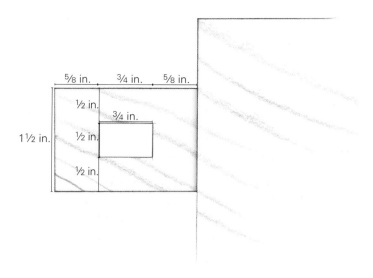

5⁄8 in.    3⁄4 in.    5⁄8 in.

1⁄2 in.

3⁄4 in.

1 1⁄2 in.   1⁄2 in.

1⁄2 in.

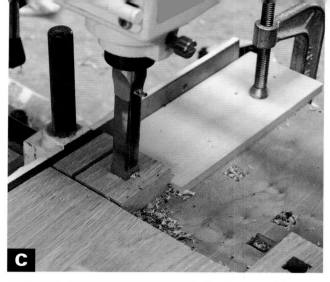

**CUT THE WEDGE MORTISES** in the tenons with a hollow-chisel mortiser. Adjust the fence to center the mortise in the tenon, and set the stop block so that the mortise will be positioned 5⁄8 in. from the end. Then move the stop block 1⁄4 in. away from the chisel to lengthen the mortise through a second cut.

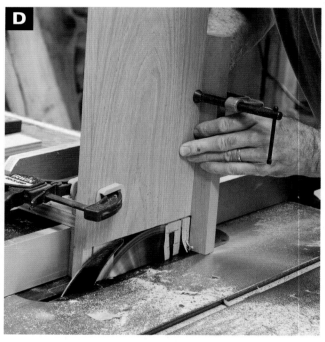

**USE A SHOPMADE TENONING JIG** to remove 1⁄8 in. from each side of the top and bottom stock to form the thickness of the 1⁄2-in. tenons. Clamp the workpiece firmly in place.

**3.** Cut the mortises in the tenons for the wedges before cutting the tenon cheeks. That way, if there's any tearout, it will be cut off. Set the fence on the mortiser so that the 1⁄2-in. mortising bit centers on each tenon, and use a stop block to control the distance from the mortise to the end of the stock. I form this mortise in two steps to get enough length for the wedges to fit tight. After making the first cut, move the stop block away from the chisel and cut again to lengthen the mortises. Refer to the drawing above to set up for this operation **(PHOTO C)**.

**4.** Hold the stock on end in a tenoning jig for cutting the cheeks of the tenons. Adjust the fence so the blade will cut 1⁄8 in. from each side. Clamp the stock securely to the tenoning jig. Cut one side, then turn the board end for end to cut the opposite side **(PHOTO D)**. Repeat on the opposite face.

**WORK SMART**

You may want to work up to the full-depth cut for the tenon cheeks to avoid cutting the tenon too thin. You can test a corner of the tenon in the mortise as you edge up to the final cut settings.

**MAKE THE FINAL TENON CUTS** with the crossscut box and sliding stop on the tablesaw.

**5.** Cut away the waste between the tenon and the end of the part on the crosscut saw. I use a sliding stop to avoid trapping the waste between the stop and blade **(PHOTO E)**.

## A SLIDING STOP BLOCK

A sliding stop block allows the stock to be perfectly positioned. The operator holds it to the left to position the stock and then slides it out of the way to prevent trapping of the waste piece. Trapping of cutoffs between the spinning blade and a stop block can cause the waste to be picked up by the blade, chewed, or thrown in the face of the operator. To set it up, slide the stop block to the left and hold it in position as you slide the center block to the right and clamp it in place to the sled. In use, hold the slide to the left against the block as you position the stock on the sled, then move it away from the stock as the cut is made.

# Make the doors and front panel

**THE BRIDLE JOINT IS DECEPTIVELY SIMPLE,** but it's one of the best ways to make doors and panels for small cabinets. Making glass doors is more complicated than making raised-panel doors because you will install the glass after assembly. As in all joinery operations, make sure all your stock is the correct thickness, width, and length.

**1.** The bridle is offset from center for ease in setup and to allow more room at the back of the frame for installing the glass and retainer strips. The front part of the bridle is $3/16$ in. thick, and the rear is $1/4$ in. thick (see the drawing on p. 82.) Use the tenoning jig shown on p. 41 or a commercial jig. A flat-tooth-grind (FTG) blade will give the best fit. After making one cut in each end, move the tenoning jig to widen the cut to the final width of $1/4$ in. **(PHOTO A)**. Note that the cuts are made 1 in. deep at the top end of each stile and $1\frac{3}{4}$ in. deep on the bottom.

**CUT THE $1/4$-IN. LEG OF THE BRIDLE. Make the first cut on the bottom end of all the stiles then lower the blade to make the cuts in the top. Adjust the distance from the blade to widen the bridle opening to $1/4$ in. This can be done in two passes using a $1/8$-in. kerf blade. Keep the front leg of the bridle on the outside.**

# Bridle joint detail

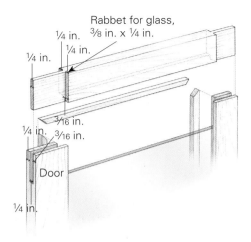

Rabbet for glass, 3/8 in. x 1/4 in.

1/4 in.

1/4 in.

1/4 in.

1/4 in.

3/16 in.

1/4 in. 3/16 in.

Door

1/4 in.

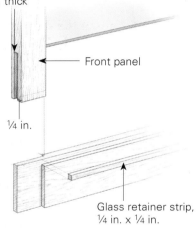

Outside bridle leg, 3/16 in. thick

Front panel

1/4 in.

Glass retainer strip, 1/4 in. x 1/4 in.

**B**

**CUT THE SHOULDERS OF THE RAIL TENONS** offset by 1/4 in. The longer shoulder on the back will fill the gap left by the rabbet for the glass. Use a stop block to set the distance from the end of the rail.

**C**

**USE A TENONING JIG TO cut the cheeks of the tenon. Cut the face on the back side first and then raise the blade height and adjust the tenoner to cut the front face. Finished joints in foreground show how these parts should fit together.**

**2.** Cut the tenon shoulders. Place a stop block on a crosscut sled and set the blade to make a 1/4-in.-deep cut 1 1/16 in. from the end of each piece on the rear face. (Note that the rail stock is long to allow trimming the tenons flush to the rails.) Then move the stop block and lower the blade to make a cut 3/16 in. deep, 1 5/16 in. from the end of the stock **(PHOTO B)**. These offset cuts result in a shoulder 1/4 in. closer to the end of the tenon at the back, filling the space left after rabbeting the stiles.

**3.** Use a tenoning jig to cut the tenon cheeks. Raise the blade so that it cuts into the shoulder cuts made in the previous step **(PHOTO C)**. Remember that the shorter tenon cheek is the front and is cut 3/16 in. from the face of the stock. The longer cheek (the back) is cut 1/4 in. from the face of the stock.

**WORK SMART**

Use scrapwood to test the fit of your parts prior to cutting joinery in your project stock. If the parts of the joint slide neatly together without force, it's a good fit. If they fall apart just from gravity alone, try again.

# Cut the rabbets for the glass

**1.** Begin cutting the rabbets for the glass on the tablesaw using the rip fence. Set the blade to make a ⅜-in.-high cut, ¼ in. from the fence. Cut on the rear face of the rail with the stock flat on the saw table. Make sure the inside edge of the rail faces the fence. Keep track of your parts in pairs, so that left and right parts will be cut on the inside edges **(PHOTO D)**. Lower the blade height to ¼ in. and move the fence to make a ⅜-in.-wide cut. Make a cut with the rear face of the rail against the fence and the inside edge on the saw table.

**2.** Cut the tenon to final height using the crosscut sled. Set the blade to cut 1⁵⁄₁₆ in. above the surface of the sled, and set the stop block to make a ¼-in.-wide cut. Clamp each piece firmly in place for this cut **(PHOTO E)**.

**SET THE TABLESAW BLADE HEIGHT AT ⅜ IN.** and the fence to make a ¼-in.-wide cut. Make sure to cut on the inside edge of the rail and the back face. Make the first cut with the stock flat on the saw table. Reset the fence to ⅜ in. and the blade height to ¼ in. and cut with the stock on edge to complete the rabbet.

**3.** Lower the blade to ¼ in. and set the sliding stop block 1⁵⁄₁₆ in. from the end of the rail to make the final cut.

**FINISH FORMING THE TENON** by using the sliding stop block on the sled. I lower the blade height to ¼ in. to remove just the last bit of waste. Sliding the stop block away from the blade during the cut prevents trapping the offcut. Then trim using the tablesaw and sled with a stop block to position the cut.

# Rout and assemble

Sand all the inside edges of each door and the front stretcher before assembly. A chamfer where the parts meet and on the inside and outside of the door frame provides an interesting detail.

**F**

**USE A 45° BIT IN THE ROUTER TABLE** to chamfer the inside edges of each door part. Set the bit height at ¹⁄₁₆ in. and test the cut using a piece of scrap wood.

**G**

**CUT CHAMFERS** where the rails meet the stiles. Use a 45° V-bit in the router table, with the fence set so that the chamfer will align with the edge of the face. Use a push block to help hold the stock at 90° to the fence.

**1.** Install a 45° chamfering bit in a table-mounted router and raise the height to ¹⁄₁₆ in. Run the outside face of the inside edge of all door and front panel parts **(PHOTO F)**.

**2.** Use a 45° pilotless router bit to chamfer the edges where the rails meet the stiles **(PHOTO G)**.

**3.** Sand these edges before assembly. To assemble the doors, simply brush glue on each tenon and add a small amount of glue to the edge of the mortises; the glue will spread as the parts are pulled tight together. Check the assembled doors and front stretcher with a square **(PHOTO H)** and then apply C-clamps to each corner.

**4.** Before assembly, rout the hinge mortises in the outer door stiles and hinge strips as shown on pp. 49–51.

**5.** You'll find that a simple sanding block will give you better control in aligning the edges of the assembled doors. Trim the bottom of the doors to the final profile, measuring up ½ in. from the bottom along the inside edge and cutting from the outside edge to this mark. Finish the outside edges with a chamfer, with the exception of the top of the front panel.

**H**

**CHECK WITH A SQUARE** that the inside corners are at exactly 90°. Then apply C-clamps at each corner to pull the bridle tight to the tenons.

# Shape the top and bottom

We left the top and bottom square to provide accurate reference surfaces for the joinery. Now that the tenons have been cut, we can cut the top and bottom to their final shape and dimensions. I use an adjustable protractor to determine the correct angle for setting up the saw.

**1.** Lay the two arms of the protractor in place at the top of the cabinet side to measure the correct angle to tilt the tablesaw blade **(PHOTO A)**. The angle of the sides of my cabinet measured about 4°, but check yours to be sure. During the process of sawing and jointing the cabinet sides, the angle on your project might turn out to be different.

**2.** Set the tablesaw to the angle from your measurement and raise the blade to ⁷⁄₈ in. high. Set the fence so that the remaining edge at the top of the cabinet will be ⁷⁄₁₆ in. and a ¼-in. ledge will be

**A**

**USE AN ANGLE FINDER** or sliding T-bevel to determine the angle of the sides. Check each corner because there may be some minor variation after bandsawing and jointing. Choose the most consistent angle for setting up for the next steps.

formed for the door to rest against in the closed position. Make the first cut with the workpiece standing on edge against the fence **(PHOTO B)**.

**3.** Lower the blade and make the second cut with the inside face of the top down flat on the saw. Lower the blade and adjust the fence so that this cut intersects cleanly with the previous cut **(PHOTO C)**.

**B**

**SET THE TABLESAW BLADE** to the same angle as the cabinet sides. Then make a cut ¾ in. deep and ⁷⁄₁₆ in. from the top edge. If your saw has a left-tilt like mine, stand the top surface against the fence for this cut. With a right-tilt saw, place the inside surface of the cabinet top against the fence.

**C**

**LOWER THE BLADE HEIGHT** and adjust the fence location so that a cut from below will intersect with the previous cut. Making sample cuts in scrap wood of equal thickness to the top will prevent mistakes.

**CUT THE EDGES OF THE BOTTOM. Raise the height of the blade but keep it at the same angle. Trim an equal amount from each edge.**

**4.** Next cut the bottom to fit. You will cut an equal amount from each side at the angle used in the previous steps. Install the cabinet top and bottom in the sides and measure from the deepest part of the cut on the top to the outside edge. Where the bottom of the cabinet fits the sides, measure from the edge and mark the cut line on each side so that it equals the measurement at the top. Measure and mark on the underside of the cabinet bottom board if you have a tablesaw with a left-tilt blade. This will make it easier to see the marks as you set up the saw. With a right-tilt saw, measure and mark the top side of the cabinet bottom board. Remember to flip the board end for end (not over) to make the second cut, so you have the angles tilting in opposite directions **(PHOTO D).**

# Prepare for assembly

**I USE THE SAME ADJUSTABLE PROTRACTOR** set at the angle from the previous steps to mark the locations for drilling the shelf support pins.

**1.** Set the protractor or sliding bevel at 4° (or the angle you determined for your project). Use it to draw lines parallel to the top and bottom 1 in. apart. Begin your guidelines 8½ in. up from the bottom of the side. Mark the centerpoint of the holes 2 in. from the edge **(PHOTO A).**

**2.** Then use the drill press to drill shelf pin holes to a depth of ½ in. on both cabinet sides **(PHOTO B).**

**USE A PROTRACTOR** set to the angle of the sides as a guide to mark the location of the shelf holes parallel to the top and bottom.

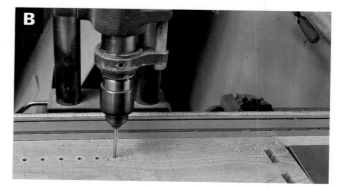

**DRILL SHELF SUPPORT HOLES** on a drill press. I set the fence to drill 2 in. from the edge of the stock and set the depth of the drill at ½ in. A brad-point bit will help in the precise location and drilling of each hole.

**CUT THE BOTTOM PROFILE** on the bandsaw, cutting from each side toward the center.

**CLAMP A GUIDE PIECE TO THE SIDE** to align the biscuit joiner. Place the clamps so that they will not interfere with the cut.

**3.** Lay out the bottom profile of the sides. Measure up ½ in. from the center. Leave the bottom flat 2 in. in from the side edges. Connect the points (see the drawing on p. 77). This relief will stabilize the cabinet on uneven surfaces as well as provide some design interest. Cut the profile on the bandsaw. Then sand the bandsaw cuts smooth **(PHOTO C)**.

**4.** Use #0 biscuits to attach the front stretcher and hinge strips to the cabinet sides. Because there might be some variation in angle on the two sides from the jointing operation, use a straightedge to align a fence to guide the biscuit joiner in the cut. Partially assemble the cabinet. Place the straightedge in the recess in the top and against the angle

in the bottom of the cabinet; then clamp a piece of wood along the side of the straightedge **(PHOTO D)**.

**5.** Mark the locations for the biscuits and then, holding the biscuit joiner base flat against the guide strip, cut the biscuit slots into the sides **(PHOTO E)**.

**6.** Mark the biscuit locations to conform to the locations on the cabinet sides and use the jointer base to index the position of the cut into the stretcher sides, as shown in **PHOTO F**.

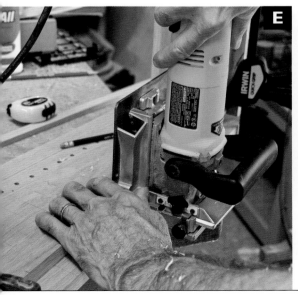

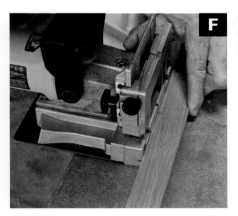

**CUT MATCHING BISCUIT SLOTS** in the stiles of the front panel and the hinge strips.

**HOLD THE BISCUIT JOINER FIRMLY** against the guide strip using the base of the joiner as your reference. You may have to reposition the clamps to gain clearance for these cuts at the different locations.

# Assemble
# and finish

**DETAILS MAKE THE DIFFERENCE.** Chamfer the edges with a 45° bit in the router before sanding. Use a block plane to chamfer the edges of the top, and a sanding block to soften the edges of the tenons where they will protrude from the sides. After these steps are complete, sand all the parts, starting with 150-grit sandpaper and working through steps to a finish sanding with 320 grit. Hand-sanding with a sanding block is the best approach if you want to maintain crisp chamfers. Also sand the doors. Cut and fit and sand the glass retainer strips.

**PUT THE WEDGES IN ONE SIDE** to hold the parts tight while you align the other side over the tenons.

**1.** Make the wedges to hold the cabinet together by making an angled cut from a ½-in.-thick white oak block. Taper the cut from ¾ in. to ⅜ in. Each blank will yield two wedges **(PHOTO A)**.

**2.** As you begin to assemble the cabinet, put the wedges in place connecting one side to the bottom and top boards, then use biscuits to locate the front stretcher. Finally, with the biscuits in place, lift the other side into place **(PHOTO B)**.

**3.** Before securing the other side with wedges, slide the front stretcher away from the top and lay a bead of glue along the top and clamp it in place **(PHOTO C)**. Tap in the wedges and leave them while the glue dries. When the glue has dried, you can mark, remove, and trim the wedges.

**CUT WEDGES FROM ½-IN. STOCK.**
The rough size is 1¼ in. × 5 in. You'll trim and shape the wedges after assembly.

It can be difficult to find hardware of the right scale and design for a cabinet of this size and so clearly identified with a specific style. I ordered the hammered pulls from a mail-order woodworking supplier.

**USE A SQUEEZE BOTTLE TO INJECT GLUE** between the cabinet top and the top edge of the front stretcher to secure the front panel.

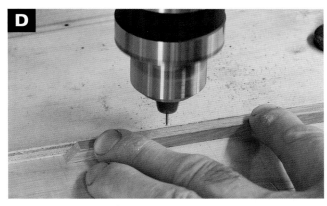

**DRILL PILOT HOLES** in the glass retainer strips before nailing them in place.

**SECURE THE GLASS RETAINER STRIPS** with ½-in. brads. A piece of cardboard over the glass helps prevent scratching.

**APPLY THE FIRST COAT** of Danish oil with a brush to get the finish into all the joints and edges. Be prepared with a dry cloth to remove and distribute excess oil.

**INSTALL THE HARDWARE.** With this pull, you'll need two drill sizes. The first hole is ¼ in. in diameter, drilled to a depth of ¼ in. Then finish by drilling through with a ³/₁₆-in. bit. Use the nails provided to attach the pulls on the bottom edges.

**4.** Drill pilot holes for the brads that secure the glass retainer strips. I use ½-in. × #20-gauge brads and use a brad mounted in the drill press as my drill bit for a precise fit. Pilot holes prevent splitting and bent nails **(PHOTO D)**.

**5.** Apply the finish before installing the glass. I use two coats of Danish oil finish and rub off the excess with a dry cloth between coats and before the oil begins to get tacky **(PHOTO E)**.

**6.** Hammer in the brads. Be sure to use a piece of thin cardboard to protect the glass **(PHOTO F)**.

**7.** Align the pulls on the center door stiles, each the same distance from the top **(PHOTO G)**.

# A contemporary variation

**I AM ALWAYS INTERESTED IN HOW SHAPES** interact and work together. I cut stock into two pieces, tapered them toward the edge, and then glued them back together and cut at an angle, causing the parts to taper in thickness toward the top. I used a biscuited miter joint where the top meets the sides to highlight the intersecting angles where the top and sides join. Shown below is the result, a classic form updated with clean, contemporary lines.

**1.** Cut the materials for the sides and top from wide planks of walnut. I used 5/4 stock due to the amount of material that must be removed from each side. Flatsawn stock with a cathedral effect gives an interesting grain pattern. Rip the stock on the bandsaw right down the middle. Plane the wood down to a common thickness and rip to equal widths of stock, removing any excess wood from the outside of the board rather than from the inside where they will be joined.

**2.** Taper the stock by making a carrier for the planer to hold the wood at an angle. Make the cut in a series of passes and remove stock from only one side. As you can see in **PHOTO A**, strips of wood attached to the carrier hold one side of the stock higher than the other.

**TAPER THE EDGE** with a shop-built carriage on the table of the planer. The carriage holds one side of the board higher than the other. Gradually increase the depth of cut in a series of passes.

MATCH THE GRAIN. This often requires shifting the parts slightly to get the perfect match. When you find it, mark where the edges meet, and mark biscuit locations.

CUT THE TOP and the top of the sides at a 45° angle on the tablesaw.

**3.** You may need to slide the parts in relation to one another to get a perfect realignment of wood grain. When the grain is aligned side to side, mark the locations for the biscuits that will join the sides to each other and the top to the sides **(PHOTO B)**.

**4.** Use the biscuit joiner to cut biscuit slots in the narrow edge of each part. Glue and clamp the two halves of each side.

**5.** Tilt the tablesaw blade at 45° to cut the top end of each side and both ends of the top **(PHOTO C)**. Then taper the sides and cut the top an equal amount from each side to match the dimension of the top.

**6.** Cut biscuit slots with the fence at 45° in the top end of the sides and in the top **(PHOTO D)**.

**7.** Because of the taper in the sides, you can't use a drill press to drill the shelf pin holes. Make a drilling template with the holes 1 in. apart. Clamp the template to the cabinet side and drill with a hand drill. To make certain that the holes align, flip the board over to drill the opposite side. I use a ¼-in. drill bit and a dowel to control the depth at ½ in. **(PHOTO E)**.

CUT THE BISCUIT SLOTS at a 45° angle in the top of the sides and the top.

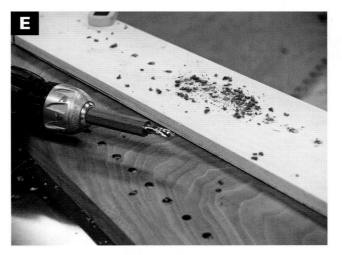

CUT THE SHELF PIN HOLES with a shopmade drilling guide to cut the holes for the shelf pins.

# Greene and Greene Cabinet

**C**HARLES AND Henry Greene were California architects who made their mark in furniture design and architecture in the first half of the 20th century. Their Arts and Crafts–era design continues to have lasting impact today. Their work often featured large finger joints to secure corners on casework. Bridle joints on doors and around panels were secured with contrasting square ebony pegs. The Greene brothers' deliberate use of exposed joinery is one reason the Greene and Greene style remains popular.

This cabinet isn't intended to duplicate a Greene and Greene piece but to explore my own interests in their design and techniques. While the exterior incorporates elements of this style, the interior is open to interpretation. With some modifications, it can be adapted to hold a variety of objects. The strong design elements suggest a masculine use for this cabinet, such as to store neckties or some favorite tools.

# Greene and Greene cabinet

In this cabinet, the joinery is exposed on the sides. The doors are built using
bridle joints like the doors in previous projects, but this time the bridle part of
the joint is in the rails, which gives the cabinet a different look. Instead of door
panels, I used a series of tongued slats.

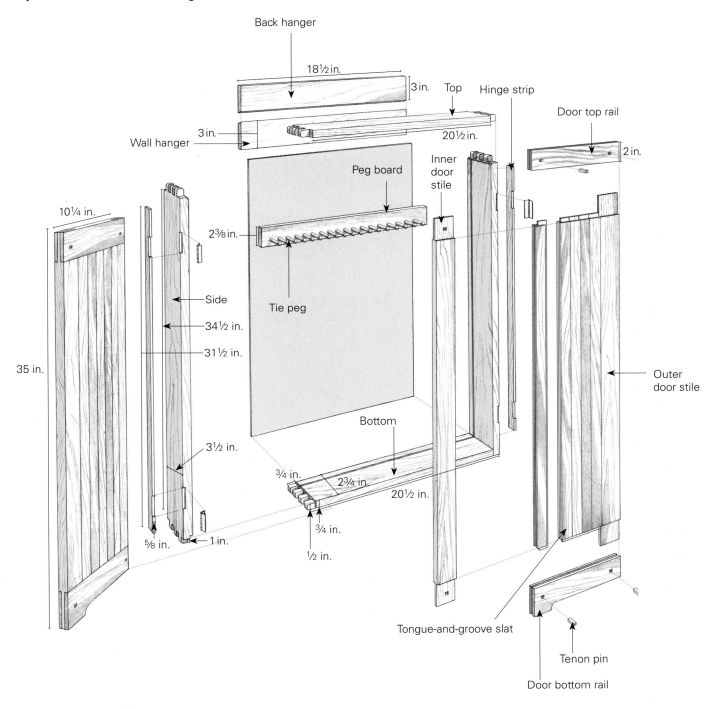

Back hanger

18½ in.

3 in.

Top

Hinge strip

Door top rail

Wall hanger

3 in.

20½ in.

2 in.

Inner door stile

Peg board

10¼ in.

2⅜ in.

Side

Tie peg

34½ in.

31½ in.

35 in.

Outer door stile

Bottom

3½ in.

¾ in.

2¾ in.

20½ in.

¾ in.

5⅛ in.

1 in.

½ in.

Tongue-and-groove slat

Tenon pin

Door bottom rail

The interior length of the cabinet is sized to accommodate half the length of a necktie plus some room top and bottom. Its depth from front to back accommodates commercially available necktie pegs. Additional brass hangers can be added to the doors to hang bolos and other items. In the tool cabinet variation, I added 2 in. in width and 1 in. in depth. I chose to outfit the interior for tools that I own but also made adjustable shelves to allow flexible storage for a variety of tools. You should adapt the interior design to fit your own tools.

You'll need a finger joint jig to cut $\frac{1}{2}$-in. × $\frac{1}{2}$-in. square fingers, long enough to be routed and exposed on the outside of the cabinet. The finger joints in Greene and Greene designs were generally square in shape, protruded beyond the cabinet sides, and were gently rounded. I chose to make the fingers $\frac{1}{2}$ in. sq. rather than the full thickness of the stock because that allowed for more of them at each corner, and by forming a rabbet joint at each corner, I was able to use the tablesaw to cut the grooves for the back.

## MATERIALS FOR GREENE AND GREENE CABINET

| QUANTITY | PART | SIZE | NOTES |
|---|---|---|---|
| 2 | Sides | $\frac{3}{4}$ in. x $3\frac{1}{2}$ in. x $34\frac{1}{2}$ in. | Elm |
| 2 | Top and Bottom | $\frac{3}{4}$ in. x $3\frac{1}{2}$ in. x $20\frac{1}{2}$ in. | Elm |
| 2 | Hinge strips | $\frac{1}{4}$ in. x $\frac{5}{8}$ in. x $31\frac{1}{2}$ in. | Elm |
| 2 | Wall hanger or hanger strip | $\frac{5}{8}$ in. x $2\frac{1}{2}$ in. x $18\frac{1}{2}$ in. | Elm |
| 1 | Back | $\frac{1}{4}$ in. x 19 in. x 33 in. | Baltic-birch plywood |
| 2 | Top door rails | $\frac{7}{8}$ in. x 2 in. x $10\frac{1}{4}$ in. | Elm |
| 2 | Bottom door rails | $\frac{7}{8}$ in. x $2\frac{1}{2}$ in. x $10\frac{1}{4}$ in. | Elm |
| 2 | Outer door stiles | $\frac{3}{4}$ in. x 2 in. x 35 in. | Elm |
| 2 | Inner door stiles | $\frac{3}{4}$ in. x $1\frac{3}{4}$ in. x 35 in. | Elm |
| 8 | Door slats (tongue and groove) | $\frac{3}{4}$ in. x $1\frac{1}{2}$ in. x $30\frac{7}{8}$ in. | Elm |
| 2 | Door slats (tongue and tongue) | $\frac{3}{4}$ in. x $1\frac{3}{4}$ in. x $30\frac{7}{8}$ in. | Elm |
| 8 | Pegs | $\frac{1}{4}$ in. x $\frac{1}{4}$ in. x $\frac{11}{16}$ in. | Walnut |
| 2 pr. | Brass hinges | 2 in. x $1\frac{3}{8}$ in. | ACE hardware #529920 |
| 2 | Tie hanger strips | $\frac{1}{2}$ in. x $2\frac{3}{8}$ in. x $18\frac{1}{2}$ in. | Hardwood or Baltic-birch plywood |
| 17 | Tie pegs | $\frac{3}{16}$ in. dia. x $\frac{3}{8}$ in. tenon, $2\frac{3}{8}$ in. length overall | Rockler #21980 |
| 2 | Wood screws | #6 x $1\frac{1}{4}$ in. | |

# Build a finger-joint jig

TO CUT FINGER JOINTS (OR BOX JOINTS) ON a tablesaw, I make a basic sled with a simple fence. I attach the guide pin to both the fence and base. These sleds are quick and easy to make and can be adapted to perform a variety of tablesaw cuts.

**1.** Cut the base to size, depending on your saw and project. I made this one 24 in. × 24 in. Then make a ¾-in.-wide groove ⅜ in. deep for the back support to fit. I find it useful to make the back support and hardwood runners in the same operation. Make the back support high enough to support the workpiece and for your hands to grasp comfortably. This one is 4 in. high overall. Plane the back board stock to fit in the groove in the base exactly.

**A**

IN THIS FINGER-JOINT JIG, two runners are cut to fit the miter gauge guide slots on the tablesaw. A groove in the plywood base holds a piece of hardwood.

**2.** Make hardwood runners to fit in the tablesaw guide slots. I plane hard maple stock down to the necessary thickness to fit the guide slot and then rip ⅜-in.-deep pieces. Cut two to the length of the plywood base, measured front to back (PHOTO A).

## A finger-joint jig

Sled-based finger-joint jigs are quick to make and can be adapted to a variety of joint sizes. The dimensions given are for context. You can make your jig any size that works for your saw and your project.

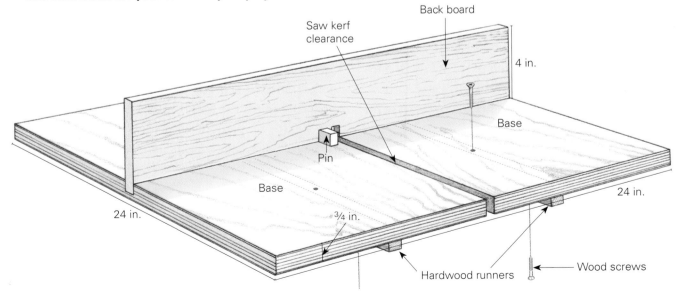

Back board

Saw kerf clearance

4 in.

Base

Pin

Base

24 in.

Base

24 in.

¾ in.

Hardwood runners

Wood screws

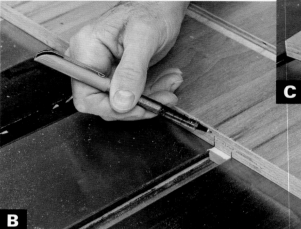

**ALIGN THE CENTER** of the plywood base to the tablesaw blade, put one guide strip in the tablesaw slot, and mark its location.

**ATTACH THE RUNNER** on the bottom with screws. Use a carpenter's square to align the runner at 90° to the front edge of the base.

**ATTACH THE SECOND RUNNER** by using screws driven from the top while the other runner is in its guide slot.

**3.** Lay the sled base on the top of the tablesaw and center it over where the blade will cut. Place the runner in the left guide slot and mark its location on the base of the sled **(PHOTO B)**.

**4.** Use a carpenter's square to square the runner on the left side with the front edge of the plywood, then countersink and install the first screw. Use the square to align the runners as the next holes are carefully drilled and the screws installed. I use 1-in.-long drywall screws so that they will not pass through to the surface **(PHOTO C)**.

**5.** Place the second runner in the miter-guide slot, turn over the base, and place the attached runner in the other slot. Drill pilot holes through the plywood into the second runner and drive 1-in. screws to secure it **(PHOTO D)**. At this point, the sled should slide back and forth with little resistance but should not move side to side.

**6.** Put the back board in the groove in the base, and install a dado blade set to a width of ½ in. in the tablesaw. (This sled will be for ½-in. fingers.) Raise the blade to about 1½ in. above the saw table. Make the first cut into the sled. Stop when the blade cuts through the back board **(PHOTO E)**.

**7.** Use a planer to size the guide pin stock to fit into the cut made in the back board. Then slide the back board over to the right until the stock fits exactly between the guide pin and the cut in the surface of the sled base. You can tell better by feel than by sight when you have adjusted the spacing for a perfect cut **(PHOTO F)**. Make a test cut. If the fingers are too loose, adjust the fit by tapping the back board very slightly to the right. If the fit is too tight, tap the back board slightly to the left.

**8.** When you are satisfied that you have a perfect fit, drive screws from underneath the sled into the back board to secure it. For safety, add a piece of wood to cover where the blade exits the rear of the back board, to remind you to keep your fingers clear of the blade.

MAKE THE FIRST CUT with a dado blade set to ½ in. wide, about 1½ in. above the saw surface.

CUT A GUIDE PIECE to fit the dado cut precisely. Slide the back board exactly ½ in. to the right. Use a scrap piece of the guide piece stock to align the back board with the left edge of the sawkerf cut with the dado blade.

# Build the sides and top

**BEGIN BY PLANING MATERIAL FOR THE** sides and top to ¾ in. thick. Then joint the edges and cut the parts to width and length.

**1.** Put the stock against the pin to make the first cut and then step the stock over the pin for each successive cut **(PHOTO A)**.

A piece of ¼-in. plywood clamped to the front face of the back board allows you to make cuts of varying heights, while preventing tearout at the back side of the cut. Make a cutout in the plywood for the pin and start with fresh backing each time you change the height of the cut.

CUT THE FINGERS on the top and bottom. Make the first cut with the stock against the guide piece and then step the stock over the guide piece after each cut.

as a spacer to hold the adjoining stock in position for the first cut. Remove the spacer to make the subsequent cuts.

**B**

**C**

CUT THE SHOULDER OF THE RABBET on the inside surfaces of the cabinet top, bottom, and sides. A tablesaw sled and stop block ensure consistent cuts.

**2.** To make the finger joints on the ends of the sides, use a piece of scrap or test-cut material as a spacer for the first cut. This spacer will position the stock so that the fingers will align properly when the joint is assembled **(PHOTO B).**

**3.** There is a rabbet on the ends to allow the ¾-in.-long finger joints to be ¼ in. proud on the outside of the cabinet. Cut the shoulder for the rabbet on a tablesaw sled, using a stop block. Raise the blade ¼ in. above the surface of the sled. The shoulder cuts on the top and bottom boards are made ¾ in. from the end of the stock **(PHOTO C).** Move the stop block ¼ in. away from the blade for the rabbet on the sides, where the shoulder is 1 in. from the end of the stock.

**4.** Use the tenoning jig on the tablesaw to finish cutting the rabbets. The space between the face of the jig and the blade is ½ in. Raise the blade to 1 in. for the sides **(PHOTO D).** Lower the blade by ¼ in. to cut the rabbets on the top and bottom. The finished parts should look like the ones in **PHOTO E.**

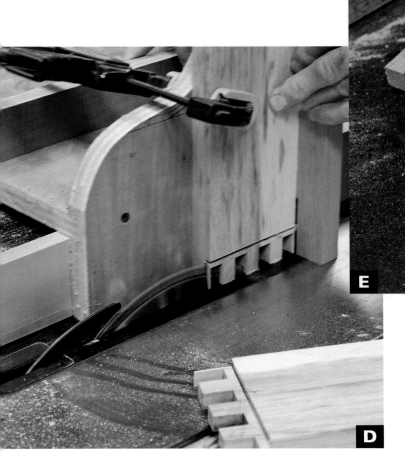

**FINISH FORMING THE RABBET JOINT** using the tenoning jig on the tablesaw. The rabbet cut is made to the height of the fingers on the top and bottom and to the thickness of the stock on the sides, leaving the fingers ½ in. × ½ in. × ¾ in. long.

**5.** Rout the ends of each finger joint using a ⅛-in. roundover bit in the router table. You will find that it works best if you secure two pieces face to face so that together they provide a larger bearing surface on the top of the router table. They will be easier to balance and control **(PHOTO F)**.

**6.** To form the groove on the top, bottom, and sides for the back panel, use a ¼-in. dado blade raised to a height of ¼ in. or a standard ⅛-in. kerf blade and make the cut in two passes to fit the thickness of the Baltic-birch plywood back. One advantage of the rabbet cut on each piece is that it provides clearance for the tablesaw blade to pass through the stock at a ¼-in. height without affecting the joints.

**7.** Glue a hinge strip on each side cabinet so that the hinged doors can swing open without interfering with the finger joints.

**USE A ⅛-IN. ROUNDOVER BIT** in the router table to rout the ends of the fingers. Clamp the sides and the top and bottom in pairs to make routing easier.

# Build the doors

**CUT THE TENONS ON THE DOOR STILES. Cut first on one side of the stock and then the other. Keep the inside face against the jig.**

**TO MAKE THE DOORS, I USE BRIDLE JOINTS** to secure the corners of the doors as in previous projects. You'll notice that my arrangement of bridles and tenons for these doors is the reverse of that used on the other projects in the book, where the bridles are on the stiles.

**AFTER USING A TENONING JIG to cut the bridle slots on the door rails, check to make sure the slot is exactly ¼ in. wide.**

**1.** After cutting the door parts to width and length, cut the bridle slot on the ends of the door rails using a tenoning jig (see p. 41). The back (inside-facing) leg of the bridle in each case is ¼ in. wide. Before cutting the tenons, use dial calipers to check the width of the bridle slot to make sure it's exactly ¼ in. **(PHOTO A)**.

**2.** Use a tablesaw sled to cut the tenon shoulders on the door to a depth of ¼ in. The tenon shoulders at the top are 2 in. from the end of the stock. At the bottom, the shoulders are 2½ in. from the end.

**3.** Cut the tenon cheeks using a tenoning jig **(PHOTO B).** The inside face is always against the jig.

## ACCURATE DOOR JOINERY

Door joinery needs to be accurate to build doors that are square and stay flat. Start with stock milled to the correct thickness, all milled at the same time. Use a tablesaw sled and stop block to ensure that all parts of the same type are of consistent length.

In this project, the rails are thicker (⅞ in.) than the stiles, which are ¾ in. thick. But it's just as easy to get a flat door with mixed dimensions. You especially want the back, which will lie against the cabinet, to be flat. The way to achieve this is to cut consistently on one face of the stock against the body of the jig. Mark your stock to keep track.

In the finished bridle, the inside legs should be consistently ¼ in. thick. The bridle slots and the tenons are also ¼ in. thick. The front legs of the bridles, which are on the rails on this project, are ⅜ in. thick.

The same is true for the ³⁄₁₆-in.-wide × ¼-in.-deep grooves that hold the slats. If you consistently run the inside (back) face of the stock against the fence, the grooves will all line up and it won't matter if your cuts aren't completely centered. With the inside face against the fence, make the first cut on both stiles and rails before making any adjustments to the fence settings. If you're using a dado, you can cut the groove in one pass.

# Greene and Greene door detail

The trick with rails and stiles of different thickness is to be consistent. Make all the cuts on the rear side of the frame members before making any adjustments to your settings to make the cuts on the front side.

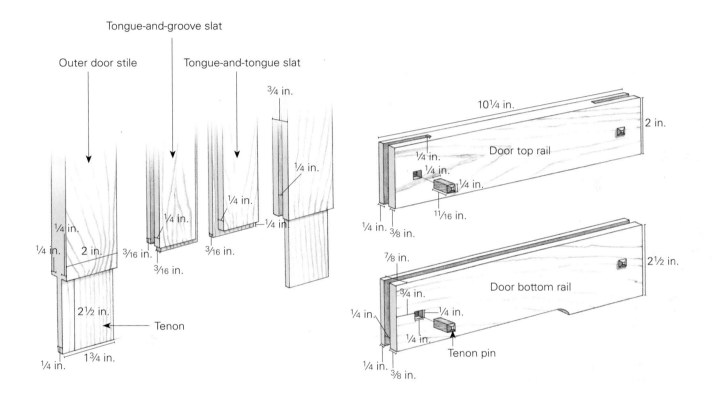

**C**

CUT THE TENONS TO WIDTH with the inside edge of the door stiles held against the tenoning jig. This cut is ¼ in. from the edge of the stock.

**D**

CUT THE SHORT SHOULDER using the crosscut sled on the tablesaw. The sliding stop block moves out of the way to prevent tapping the off cut.

**4.** Make the first cut using the tablesaw and tenoning jig with the blade ¼ in. from the body of the jig as shown in **PHOTO C**.

**5.** Use the sled and sliding stop block to make the final shoulder cuts **(PHOTO D)**.

## Cut the grooves and make the slats

**E**

HOLD THE STOCK ON EDGE (inside edge down) to cut the grooves in the door frame parts. Hold the inside (rear) face of the stiles and rails against the fence.

**1.** Mill the slat stock to ¾ in. thickness and cut them to consistent width on the tablesaw. Note that the tongue-and-tongue slats are ¼ in. wider than the tongue-and-groove slats because there is a tongue on both sides.

**2.** Cut the ³⁄₁₆-in. grooves in the door stiles and rails. For this cut, you can use a ³⁄₁₆-in. dado blade or a standard ⅛-in. blade and move the fence over ¹⁄₁₆ in. to widen the cuts. Set the blade height for a ¼-in.-deep cut. Make all the cuts with the inside face (the rear face) of the stiles and rails against the fence **(PHOTO E)**. If you're using a standard blade, make the first cut on all parts, including the grooves in the slats, before making adjustments to widen the kerf to ³⁄₁₆ in.

F

**ADJUST THE TABLE-SAW FENCE** after cutting the groove on one side of the slats to cut the 3/16-in.-wide × 1/4-in.-deep tongues. The first two cuts are on edge. The second cuts are with the stock flat on the saw table.

**3.** Cut the grooves on the tongue-and-groove slats using the same setup you used to cut the grooves for the interior parts of the doors.

**4.** Cut the tongue parts on the other side of the stock. Each tongue requires four cuts. The first two cuts are on edge with the blade set at the same height as for the groove. The second two cuts are with the stock flat on the saw table. The fence is set to make a 1/4-in.-wide cut. Use the kerfs you just cut to determine the height of the cut **(PHOTO F)**.

**5.** Shape the edges of the tongue-and-groove parts by using a 1/8-in. roundover router bit in the router table. Raise the height of the bit so its cut aligns with the bottom edge of the flat face of the stock. Then lower the router bit to cut even with the surface of the router table **(PHOTO G)**.

**6.** Trim the tongue-and-groove stock to length using the tablesaw sled. The stop block controls the length of the cut.

**7.** Use the tablesaw and stop block to cut the short tenons on each end of the slats. Set the blade height to the height of the tongue and the stop block to control the tongue's length at 1/4 in. After making the first cut with the stock against the stop block, back it away 1/8 in. to remove the remaining waste **(PHOTO H)**.

**ROUND THE EDGES** of the tongue-and-groove parts with a 1/4-in. roundover bit. Rout the grooved edge flush with the surface, and raise it 1/4 in. above the surface to rout the tongued side.

G

H

**FORM THE TENONS** on the end of the stock using the sled and stop block. Set the blade height to the height of the groove and set the distance from the stop block to the outside of the cut at 1/4 in.

## Shape and assemble the doors

**8.** To form the shape at the bottom of the doors, use a 1¼-in.-dia. straight-cut router bit in the router table. Set up stops to control the length of travel, stopping short of the ends as shown in **PHOTO I**. Raise the router bit in increments for this operation, taking off just a bit at a time. Leave an edge as shown to give a bearing surface against the fence. Remove the waste with a rasp. An easy alternate for this technique would be to use the bandsaw.

**9.** Round over the edges of the rails with a ⅛-in. roundover bit.

**10.** Assemble the doors. To assemble the tongue-and-groove doors, align the tongue-and-groove parts with the tongue-and-tongue piece at the center. Then put the stiles in place. Spread glue on the tenons, and then slide the rails into place. Apply pressure on the outside of each joint with C-clamps. Wooden pads between the clamps and wood distribute the clamping pressure and prevent marring the wood. Check the assembly for square.

**SHAPE THE BOTTOM EDGE** of the lower rails with a 1¼-in.-dia. router bit mounted in the router tables. Place stops to control the travel of the parts on the table and raise the cutter in a series of steps to its full height, leaving just a bit remaining to give it a secure relationship to the fence. This remaining edge can be removed with a rasp.

# Assemble the carcase

**CUT THE BACK PANEL** from ¼-in.-thick Baltic-birch plywood.

**BEFORE ROUTING THE HINGE MORTISES,** assemble the carcase. Have lots of clamps on hand of the right length. Use a needle-nose glue squeeze bottle to inject glue between the fingers of the joint.

**1.** Cut the back panel to dimension on the tablesaw **(PHOTO A)**. Then sand it smooth. Check that the edges will fit easily in the grooves cut in the top, bottom, and sides. If necessary, do some sanding on the edges to get it to fit without the need to force it.

USE A SQUEEZE BOTTLE to apply glue to the inside surfaces of the finger joints as they are pushed together. Apply the glue carefully to avoid cleanup. If the joint is a tight fit, a small amount of glue will suffice.

**2.** To glue the corners of the cabinet without making a mess, I partially assemble the joints, and then spread glue with a squeeze bottle on only the inside surfaces of the joints **(PHOTOS B, C)**.

**3.** Use clamps to pull all the corners tight **(PHOTO D)**. Check to make sure the assembly is square. Allow the glue to dry thoroughly.

BAR CLAMPS HOLD THE TOP, bottom, and sides tightly together as the glue sets. Use a square to make certain that the assembly is square before leaving it to dry.

# Hinge and trim the doors

**A HINGE-ROUTING TEMPLATE** makes it easy to rout the hinge mortise in the cabinet sides and doors.

**THERE ARE SEVERAL WAYS TO CUT THE** hinge mortises. You can do it by hand as shown on pp. 17–19. Or you can use a router template as shown on pp. 49–51.

**1.** Construct a hinge mortise template of the appropriate size **(PHOTO A)** and use a top-bearing bit to rout the mortise.

**2.** You can use a tablesaw to trim the edges where the bridle joint overlaps or protrudes (see p. 48). Or use a router with a bearing at the top. This is the same kind of bearing I used for routing the hinge mortise. The bearing follows the edge and removes waste **(PHOTO B)**.

**WORK SMART**

Always measure the thickness of the hinge carefully to cut the mortise to the right depth. Otherwise the door may bind. If it does, you'll need to adjust the depth of the mortise by recutting or shimming the mortise with veneer or pieces of cardboard.

**THE SAME KIND OF** top-piloted straight-cut router bit used to cut the hinge mortise can trim the tenon protruding on the outside of the doors. For the shaped bottom rail, this is a more controlled method.

# Pin the doors

**JOINTS PINNED WITH EBONY PEGS ARE A** distinctive Greene and Greene design element. Since ebony sells for many dollars a pound, and I like working with local woods, I substitute ebonized walnut for the real thing.

**1.** Use a hollow-chisel mortiser to cut ¼-in.-sq. holes in the corners of each door, centered on the rails. Clamp the door firmly in place and adjust the depth of the mortiser so that the hole goes only partway through **(PHOTO A)**. This will allow you to better control the height that the pin protrudes on the outside of the door. You can also cut the mortises by hand by drilling away some of the waste with a slightly undersize drill bit and squaring up the hole with a chisel.

**2.** Mill walnut stock to fit the mortises in the doors. Then use a tablesaw sled to cut the walnut pieces to length. I use a sliding stop block to prevent trapping and use the eraser end of a pencil to give additional support during the cut. The eraser also comes in handy for moving the part away from the fence for the next cut **(PHOTO B)**.

**A**

**USE A ¼-IN. MORTISING CHISEL to cut square holes for the pegs.**

**3.** Sand one end of the pegs on each edge to form a four-sided chamfer.

**4.** Treat the walnut pegs with an ebonizing solution made from a cup of common household vinegar with a pad of #0000 steel wool partially dissolved in it. Brush the liquid on the top of each walnut peg and let it dry. A second application will give the deepest black. Leave the bottom untreated for the best glue surface.

**5.** Put just a dab of glue in the mortises and tap the pegs in place using a block of wood as a cushion to prevent marring the top of the peg **(PHOTO C)**.

**B**

**CUT ¼-IN.-SQ. STOCK TO LENGTH on the tablesaw. I shape the ends with a four-sided chamfer using a belt sander before cutting the pegs to final length.**

**C**

**DRIVE THE PEGS using a light hammer and a hardwood block to protect the chamfered end from being marred.**

# Install the tie hanger

**BEFORE INSTALLING THE TIE HANGER, MAKE** matching strips to hang the cabinet to the wall, as shown on p. 49. One strip is glued on the cabinet's back panel; the other is screwed to the wall. The two strips are cut from a single piece of stock cut at a 35° angle. Use clamps and glue to attach it. I use wood blocks on the inside and a block of wood at the back to spread the clamping pressure.

**1.** Make the tie hanger from a piece of elm and drill holes spaced 1 in. apart for hanging ties. Plane the stock to a thickness of ½ in. and rout one edge with a ⅛-in. roundover bit.

**2.** Use a drill press to drill the ³⁄₁₆-in. × ⅜-in.-deep holes for the hanger pegs.

**3.** Put a dab of glue in each hole and use a tack hammer to tap the pegs into place **(PHOTO A)**.

**4.** After the pegs are in place, clamp the hanger strip tightly to the inside of the cabinet. Predrill and countersink and drive 1¼-in. screws in from behind **(PHOTO B)**.

**5.** Sand all exposed parts not previously sanded. Apply your choice of finish. I chose Danish oil, which is very forgiving. Install the hinges and a stop with magnetic door catches (see p. 51), and the tie cabinet is complete.

**PUT A DAB OF GLUE** into each hole and use a light hammer to tap the tie pegs into place.

**CLAMP THE TIE HANGER** in place using blocks to achieve the depth. Drive 1¼-in. screws through the back hanger strip to secure the tie hanger.

# A tool-cabinet alternative

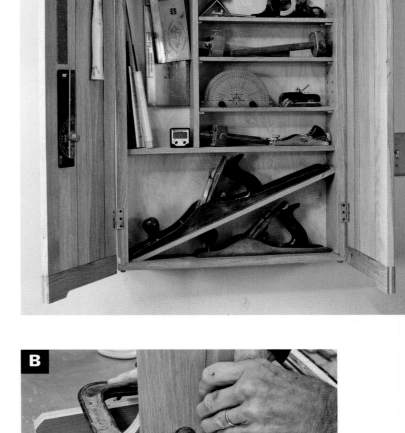

**THIS TOOL CABINET VARIATION IS BUILT IN** the same way, except it's 1 in. deeper and 2 in. wider, a better size to accommodate tools. The extra depth allows me to hang marking and measuring tools on the doors and leaves space for a vertical compartment to hang dovetail saws. In my original design, I had forgotten my Stanley® #07 plane, which could have used a couple more inches in cabinet width. But it proved to be an opportunity to be creative. I made an angled shelf for the #07 plane and that left a space below it, just right for my #05.

**1.** To lay out the design of the interior, arrange the tools in their storage positions. In **PHOTO A** I'm checking the angle so that I can use it to set up the saw to cut the shelf for the #07 plane.

**2.** The first angled cut is made with the tablesaw and tenoning jig **(PHOTO B)**, and the second on the other end of the shelf is made with the saw tilted to the same angle but using the standard miter gauge instead.

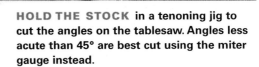

**HOLD THE STOCK** in a tenoning jig to cut the angles on the tablesaw. Angles less acute than 45° are best cut using the miter gauge instead.

**TO PLAN THE INTERIOR** of the tool cabinet, place the tools in relation to one another as they will be stored in the cabinet. Because my jointer plane is too long for the width of the cabinet, I'll make an angled shelf, and use a protractor to determine the correct angle.

**POCKET HOLE SCREWS** secure the angled shelf to the cabinet sides. A block of wood clamped to the cabinet side helps keep the shelf in position as the screws are driven into place.

**FOR ADJUSTABLE SHELVES** in part of the cabinet, use a drilling guide to accurately position the holes on both sides.

**3.** Pocket screws offer an ideal way to secure the shelves and dividers on the inside of the tool cabinet. They're quick to install and can easily be removed if you want to reconfigure the interior of the cabinet later. Use a pocket-hole drilling guide to drill the holes in the parts for the shelves and dividers. You will find it helpful to clamp temporary blocking in place to help position interior parts as the pocket screws are driven in place **(PHOTO C)**.

**4.** To add adjustable shelves, make a drilling guide and depth stop for your drill. Clamp the drilling guide in place and drill each hole for shelf pins to fit. On the shelves, I plan to put a variety of smaller planes and marking gauges, so the ability to adjust the distance between shelves is useful **(PHOTO D)**.

# Jelly Cabinet

**T**HIS JELLY CABINET is based on one I made for a customer many years ago. I've called this project a jelly cabinet because storing jams and jellies would be a traditional use for a small cabinet like this. But you could also use it to house wine, plates, or other household objects.

The construction techniques are fairly simple. I used biscuit joints to connect the panels that make up the side, front, and back. Tongue-and-groove units form the bottom, fixed shelf, and top. I built the door frames using bridle joints and used maple panels to provide contrast with the surrounding cherry.

Seven basic subassemblies make up this cabinet: the sides, back, front, bottom, shelf, and top. I make the sides, front, and back first and then cut the parts for the bottom, fixed-shelf, and top after the other assemblies are complete. This allows me to double-check the actual dimensions as I work and to make any necessary adjustments for a perfect fit.

# Jelly cabinet

This cabinet looks complicated, but it uses straightforward biscuit joinery to hold the carcase panels together. Mark all parts carefully to keep track of them during construction and assembly.

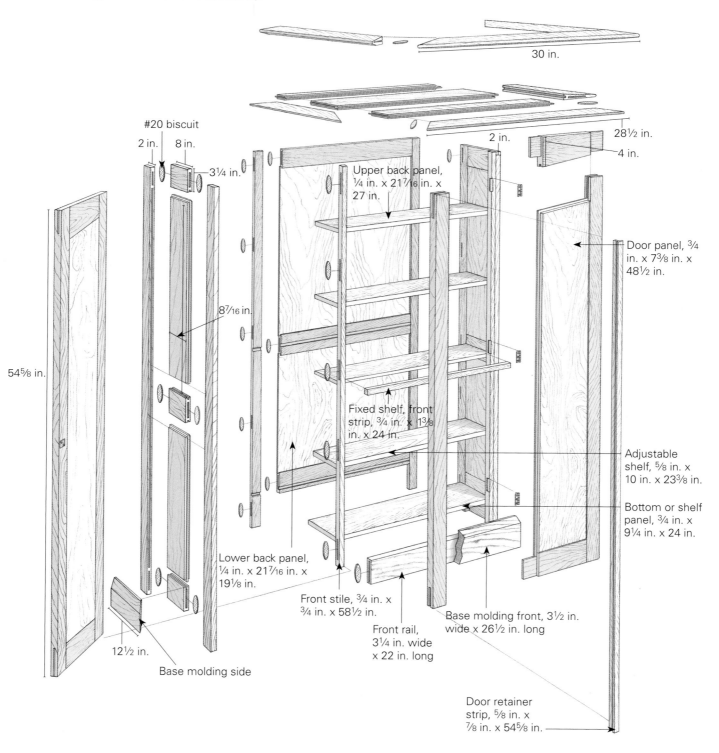

30 in.

#20 biscuit

2 in.   8 in.

3¼ in.

28½ in.

2 in.

4 in.

Upper back panel, ¼ in. x 21⁷⁄₁₆ in. x 27 in.

Door panel, ¾ in. x 7³⁄₈ in. x 48½ in.

8⁷⁄₁₆ in.

Fixed shelf, front strip, ¾ in. x 1³⁄₈ in. x 24 in.

Adjustable shelf, ⁵⁄₈ in. x 10 in. x 23³⁄₈ in.

Bottom or shelf panel, ¾ in. x 9¼ in. x 24 in.

54⁵⁄₈ in.

Lower back panel, ¼ in. x 21⁷⁄₁₆ in. x 19⅛ in.

Front stile, ¾ in. x ¾ in. x 58½ in.

Front rail, 3¼ in. wide x 22 in. long

Base molding front, 3½ in. wide x 26½ in. long

12½ in.

Base molding side

Door retainer strip, ⁵⁄₈ in. x ⁷⁄₈ in. x 54⁵⁄₈ in.

# MATERIALS FOR JELLY CABINET

| QUANTITY | PART | SIZE | NOTES |
|---|---|---|---|
| **CARCASE COMPONENTS** | | | |
| 4 | Side stiles | ¾ in. x 2 in. x 58½ in. | Cherry |
| 6 | Side rails | ¾ in. x 3¼ in. x 8 in. | Cherry |
| 2 | Side lower panels | ¾ in. x 8⁷⁄₁₆ in. x 19⁹⁄₁₆ in. | Cherry |
| 2 | Side upper panels | ¾ in. x 8⁷⁄₁₆ in. x 27 in. | Cherry |
| 2 | Back stiles | ¾ in. x 1¼ in. x 58½ in. | Cherry |
| 3 | Back rails | ¾ in. x 3¼ in. x 21 in. | Cherry |
| 1 | Back lower panel | ¼ in. x 21⁷⁄₁₆ in. x 19⅛ in. | Baltic-birch plywood |
| 1 | Back upper panel | ¼ in. x 21⁷⁄₁₆ in. x 27 in. | Baltic-birch plywood |
| 2 | Front stiles | ¾ in. x ¾ in. x 58½ in. | Cherry |
| 1 | Front rail | ¾ in. x 3¼ in. x 22 in. | Cherry |
| **TOP** | | | |
| 1 | Top front | ¾ in. x 2½ in. x 25½ in. | Cherry |
| 1 | Top back | ¾ in. 2¼ in. x 25½ in. | Cherry |
| 1 | Top panel | ¾ in. 9¼ in. x 24 in. | Cherry |
| **BOTTOM AND SHELVES** | | | |
| 2 | Bottom or fixed shelf fronts | ¾ in. x 1⅜ in. x 24 in. | Cherry |
| 2 | Bottom or fixed shelf panels | ¾ in. x 9¼ in. x 24 in. | Cherry |
| 3 | Adjustable shelves | ⅝ in. x 10 in. x 23⅜ in. | Cherry |
| **DOORS** | | | |
| 4 | Door stiles | ¾ in. x 2 in. x 54⅝ in. | Cherry |
| 2 | Door upper rails | ¾ in. x 4¼ in.* x 11 in. | Cherry |
| 2 | Door lower rails | ¾ in. x 3¼ in. x 11 in. | Cherry |
| 2 | Door panels | ¾ in. x 7⅜ in. x 48½ in.† | Maple |
| 1 | Door retainer strip | ⅝ in. x ⅞ in. x 54⅝ in. | Cherry |

*Preliminary width; cut to final width after tenons are formed. †Preliminary length; mark and cut the angle at the top from trial-door assembly.

## MATERIALS (CONTINUED)

| QUANTITY | PART | SIZE | NOTES |
|---|---|---|---|
| **MOLDINGS** | | | |
| 2 | Crown sides (lower) | 7/8 in. x 1¾ in. x 13¾ in. | Cherry |
| 1 | Crown front (lower) | 7/8 in. x 1¾ in. x 28½ in. | Cherry |
| 2 | Crown sides (upper) | 7/8 in. x 1¾ in. x 14⅝ in. | Cherry |
| 1 | Crown front (upper) | 7/8 in. x 1¾ in. x 30 in. | Cherry |
| 2 | Base sides | 11/16 in. x 3½ in. x 12½ in. | Cherry |
| 1 | Base front | 11/16 in. x 3½ in. x 26½ in. | Cherry |
| **OTHER MATERIALS** | | | |
| 2 | Door pulls | 1⅛ in. dia. | Hammered iron; Horton Brasses #BK-8 |
| 3 pr. | Ball-tip hinges | 2 in. x 1⅜ in. (open width) | Antique brass; Ace Hardware #S499995 |
| 34 | Biscuits | #20 | For carcase components |
| 4 | Biscuits | #0 | For crown molding |
| 12 | Shelf brackets | ¼ in. | Woodcraft #27116 |
| 13 | Wood screws | #6 x 1¼ in. | Steel |

## DEALING WITH MULTIPLE ASSEMBLIES

As projects become larger, and particularly when made from solid wood, they also become more complicated. While solid hardwood sides are fine for a very small cabinet, a larger cabinet is better able to accommodate seasonal wood expansion and contraction when the carcase is built using frame-and-panel subassemblies.

The actual skills required to build this cabinet are within a beginning craftsman's easy reach, but the complexity of dealing with a large number of parts of varying dimensions can be daunting. Managing so many parts and keeping them in order requires a strategy. Carefully marking parts helps, but even more important is building one type of assembly at a time.

One of the things that woodworkers learn from experience is to build from actual measurements taken as they work rather than those laid out in a cutlist or plan. That way, adjustments can be made as the construction progresses. So, while I offer a cutlist with this project, small variations in how you measure and cut can have a big impact on how the parts fit together.

Work in sections, building like assemblies. For instance, make the framework for the sides and double-check the dimensions for the panels and adjust the fit if necessary. Then make the bottom, shelf, and top based on the actual finished dimensions taken from the sides. In other words, don't start out by cutting all the parts to size based on the cutlist, but rather proceed in sections and double-check dimensions as you go. This strategy will give better results in your finished work and avoid miscut parts and wasted wood.

# Build the frames

**BEGIN BY JOINTING AND PLANING THE** stock for the stiles and rails for the sides, front, and back. Choose the straightest stock for the stiles. These parts need to be made from stock without knots or other imperfections. This is particularly important for the door stiles to keep the doors flat in the finished cabinet.

**1.** Carefully lay out the centerlines for the biscuits in the stiles of the sides, front, and back. Set the biscuit joiner fence to cut in the center of the ¾-in. stock and to the depth for #20 biscuits. Secure the work with clamps to prevent movement while cutting the slots **(PHOTO A)**.

**2.** Follow the same procedure for cutting the biscuit slots in the ends of the rails **(PHOTO B)**.

**CUT SLOTS** for #20 biscuits in the side rails with a biscuit joiner.

**MARK THE CENTERS** of each end of the rails and cut biscuit slots. Secure the wood to the workbench with a clamp.

**CUT THE GROOVES** in the stiles using a ¼-in. winged slot cutter in the router table. Mark entry and exit points to indicate where to stop and start the cut, avoiding the area of the biscuit slots.

**ROUT THE RAIL GROOVES** using the same setup. Note that the center parts get grooved on both sides while the parts for the top and bottom of the sides are only grooved on one side.

**3.** Cut the grooves for the raised panels to fit the sides by using a winged slot cutter in the router table. This cutter is designed to cut a ¼-in.-wide groove in the edge of the stock with the depth of cut controlled either by the size of the bearing or the placement of the fence. Choose a bearing and set the fence so the cutter makes a groove ¼ in. deep on the edge of the stock. Adjust the height of the cutter so that it is centered in the ¾-in. stock. To keep the groove from interfering with the biscuit slots, make start and stop marks in pencil to correspond with the ends of the biscuit slot. Rout between them, thereby avoiding the biscuit slots. Push the stock into the cut at the start line and then pull it away from the cutter when you reach the stop line **(PHOTO C)**.

**4.** Rout grooves in the rails at the same setting. The rails at the top and bottom have a groove only on the inside edge, while the center rails must be grooved on both edges **(PHOTO D)**.

**WORK SMART**

Mark your panel frame members to indicate which side is out. Then always rout with one face down on the table (either front or back, but be consistent). That way, even if your bit height isn't completely centered on the part, the grooves in the frame will all match up after assembly.

# Make the carcase panels

**GLUE UP THE PANELS** from narrower stock. Take care in aligning wood grain. Plane roughsawn wood to $^{13}/_{16}$ in. thick, then, after the glue has dried, plane it to the final thickness of $^{3}/_{4}$ in.

**PLANE THE MATERIAL FOR THE PANELS TO** a preliminary thickness of $^{13}/_{16}$ in. to $^{7}/_{8}$ in. and joint the edges so they fit tight. Cherry has some natural variation in color and grain pattern. You may have some trouble finding a perfect match, but move the stock around until you find the most pleasing configuration.

**1.** Glue up the panels from narrower stock (**PHOTO A**) unless full-width stock is available. After the glue has set, plane the side panels down to $^{3}/_{4}$ in. and cut them to width and length. See the sidebar below for the formula to determine panel width.

**2.** Set the tablesaw blade height to $^{1}/_{4}$ in. and cut along the edge of each raised panel with the blade $^{1}/_{4}$ in. from the fence, with the face and then with the back side flat on the tablesaw. Make your first cuts with the short grain against the fence.

**3.** Then make the same cuts on both sides with the long edges against the fence (**PHOTO B**).

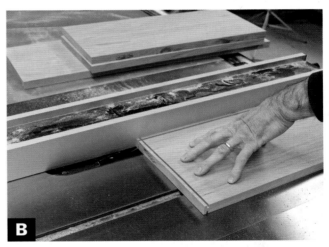

**B**

**CUT THE SHOULDERS FOR THE TONGUES** on the edges of each panel. Make the short grain cuts first to reduce tearout. Then cut the long-grain sides.

## SIZING PANELS

Panels shrink and expand with changes in moisture. If tolerances are too close, panels can actually push the frame joints apart. To size panels for this cabinet or others, begin by determining the moisture level of the wood, making sure it is sufficiently dry. You also need to size the panel to allow it to move as it expands and contracts in response to seasonal changes in moisture.

Begin by measuring the length of the rails, exclusive of tenon length. Add to that the depth of the two grooves cut in the door rails to house the panel tongues. Then subtract approximately $^{1}/_{32}$ in. for each 4 in. of panel width. As an example, this cherry cabinet has rails 8 in. long. Take the 8 in. plus $^{1}/_{2}$ in. for the tongues, less $^{1}/_{16}$ in. to allow for expansion, and you'll get a width of $8^{7}/_{16}$ in.

Fortunately, wood significantly expands and contracts only across the grain, so the length is less critical. However, I always cut panels $^{1}/_{64}$ to $^{1}/_{32}$ in. shorter than the necessary length. This leaves some clearance and prevents problems during assembly.

**REMOVE THE WASTE** by cutting on the edges of the panels, standing the stock flat against the fence.

**4.** To finish forming the tongues, make cuts into the end of the stock with the panels held vertically against the fence **(PHOTO C)**. A zero-clearance table-saw insert gives support to the stock during the cut. A featherboard helps hold the wood tightly against the fence for better control.

**5.** For a precise fit, make both cuts to finish forming the tongue with the same side of the stock against the fence. Make the second cut after moving the fence so that the opening between the blade and fence is ½ in. and the resulting tongue is ¼ in. thick. I use scrap wood to make a test cut for fit before I make my final cuts on the panels. This allows me to adjust the cut for a perfect fit. Use a cutoff from one of the rails to check the fit of the tongue **(PHOTO D)**.

**6.** When you're satisfied with the fit of the panel tongue in the groove, proceed to form the tongues around the perimeter of each panel **(PHOTO E)**.

**USE A SCRAP** of rail stock to fine tune the fit of the panel in the groove.

## WORK SMART

Keep the same side of the stock against the fence. Adjust the fence distance rather than flip the work-piece to cut the opposite side of each tongue. That way all tongues will be the same thickness and the same distance from the panel face.

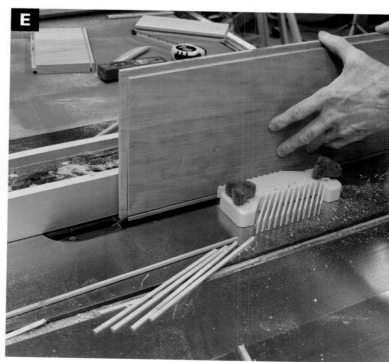

**CONTINUE FORMING THE TONGUES** on the long-grain sides with the panel on edge.

# Complete the carcase assemblies

**ROUTING THE FRAMES AND PANELS GIVES** them more visual interest. I use a 45° chamfering bit to rout the edges of the rails and stiles. Then I rout the raised panel edges with a V-groove bit.

**1.** Rout both outside edges of the center rails and the inside edge of the top and bottom rails. I set the height of the cut so that approximately ⅛ in. of the cutting surface is exposed. I also use a fence with this operation to keep the cutter away from my hands **(PHOTO A)**.

**2.** To rout the stiles, assemble the side, front, and back units without the panels in place. Use bar clamps to secure the parts tightly in position with dry biscuits in place to hold everything in alignment. Then use the same chamfering router bit in a hand-held router to rout the edges of the stiles and rout into the corners. The bearing will stop the router travel at the right place.

**USE A 45° CHAMFERING BIT** mounted in the router table to rout the inside edges of the rails and stiles.

**3.** Finish the chamfer in the corner using a straight chisel; first cut along the routed plane on the rails, then cut from the other direction. Taking thin shavings with a very sharp chisel will work better than trying to take a large cut **(PHOTO B)**.

**ASSEMBLE THE FRAME** with dry biscuits and hold it together with clamps. Use a hand-held router with a 45° chamfering bit to rout the inside edges. Cut from both sides with a sharp chisel to finish the corner cut.

**CUT A MATCHING CHAMFER** on the panel with a V-groove bit. Position the router-table fence and bit height so that the chamfers on the panel and frame match.

**4.** Rout the panel edges. Use a V-groove router bit to form the edges of the raised panels. This operation could also be done with a block plane, but in either case form the chamfer on the end grain first. Adjust the position of the router-table fence and the height of the cut so that the chamfer aligns with that cut in the horizontal stretchers as shown in **PHOTO C**. Use your test piece from forming the panel tongues to make test cuts for this operation before cutting your project stock.

## Glue and assemble the sides, back, and front

**PUT GLUE AND BISCUITS IN THE SLOTS.**
Assemble the frames and panels and clamp the assemblies as the glue sets.

**1.** Cut the back panels to size from ¼-in.-thick plywood.

**2.** Sand all the panels and the inside edges of all the frame parts before assembly.

**3.** Insert glue and biscuits in the vertical stretchers, and then in the ends of the horizontal stretchers. When making an assembly with biscuits, the parts can misalign, so watch closely to make certain the parts are lined up exactly where you want them as you tighten the clamps **(PHOTO D)**.

**4.** Assemble the front frame. Glue and clamp it.

## GETTING THE GLUE-UP RIGHT

Glue-ups can be hectic, so being prepared is a good idea. Have a block of wood and hammer handy to tap the parts into alignment. Alignment of the center rail depends on the panel size. If you get the top and bottom rails in place and the panels are the right length, the center rail will be in the right place.

Slight misalignments of the center rail can be resolved by tapping the whole assembled unit on the floor to shift the position of the parts.

But you can make such adjustments only before the glue sets.

Apply clamps at each end and at the center stretcher to pull the joints tight. Use a tape measure to check from corner to corner that the assembly is square, or use a carpenter's square to see that the bottom and sides are 90° to each other. Clamp the parts for at least 45 minutes before going on to the next operation.

# Rout grooves for the bottom and fixed shelf

**USE A STRIP OF WOOD** to serve as a fence to guide the router. The grooves are cut with a ½-in. spiral bit set to a depth of ¼ in. Mark start and stop points for the router so the grooves will not be visible on the outside of the cabinet.

**THE GROOVES ON THE BACK** can be routed through the edge because the side panels will hide where the groove exits the stiles.

**1.** Mark the location of the groove from the top and bottom, ½ in. from the bottom edge of the bottom rail and the same distance from the top edge of the top rail for the sides. The grooves for the shelves are centered on the middle rail. Measure the distance from the outside of the router bit to the edge of the router base. This will give you the distance from the bottom end of the stock to the location for the guide strip.

**2.** Clamp the fence and the cabinet parts to the workbench so they won't move. Rout from left to right so that the direction of the router rotation pulls the router toward the guide strip. Note in **PHOTO E** that the grooves cut in the sides have starting and stopping points to hide the groove from the outside of the cabinet. Start and stop your grooves ½ in. to ⅝ in. from the edges of the cabinet side assemblies. The endpoints of the groove will be covered by the front and back assembly, so they need not be chiseled square.

**3.** Use the same technique for routing the grooves in the back, but you can rout a through groove because the sides will cover the groove **(PHOTO F)**.

**WORK SMART**

Allowing the bottom, top, and shelf to float in grooves in the carcase provides some room for seasonal expansion and contraction and also gives the cabinet additional structural rigidity. To rout the grooves, I use ½-in. upcut-spiral router bit because it clears the waste better and produces a smoother cut.

## Cut the biscuit slots

**1.** Mark the location for each of the biscuits in the front, back, and side assemblies. Use five biscuits in each corner, making your marks from the bottom edge of each unit. Space the biscuits equally, one at each end, one in the center, and one between each end and the center. Set the fence depth so that the front and back will be slightly inset from the outer edges of the sides by ⅛ in. This reveal adds visual interest at the corners of the cabinet and eliminates the need for the edges to be aligned perfectly.

**2.** Set the biscuit joiner for #20 biscuits and cut the slots for the biscuits that attach the back assembly and the front stretcher to the sides.

**3.** You may find it a bit awkward to cut the biscuit slots in the sides. Hold the unit on edge with clamps as shown in **PHOTO G**.

**CLAMPS HOLD THE CABINET SIDES** on edge, making it easier to cut the biscuit slots. Offset the biscuit location so that the front and back are inset ⅛ in. from the sides.

## Prepare the front for the base molding

**CLEAN UP THE NOTCH** for the base molding with a sharp chisel. You can rough out the notch on the tablesaw with the blade raised to ⅛ in. and a stop block positioned to make the first cut at 3½ in. from the blade.

**1.** Sand the sides, back, front stretcher, and shelves through a progression of grits. I start with a random-orbit sander with 150-grit sandpaper and move up to a final sanding with 320 grit.

**2.** Cut a 3½-in.-high ⅛-in.-deep recess across the front of the cabinet sides to provide a place for the base molding to fit tightly against the front rail. This small cut is important because it allows for the cabinet sides to extend beyond the front stretcher without needing a strip to fill a gap where the base molding is to be attached later. Rough out the cut using a sled on the tablesaw with the blade raised to a height of ⅛ in. Make the first cut with the bottom end of the cabinet side against the stop block set 3½ in. from the blade. Nibble the stock away in a series of cuts. Remove any remaining waste with a sharp chisel (**PHOTO H**).

# Make the top, bottom, and shelf

**I CHOSE TO USE TONGUE-AND-GROOVE** construction for these parts to keep the panels flat but also to allow the wood to move with seasonal moisture changes. With the exception of the top, these units have a ½-in.-thick × ¼-in.-long tongue on three sides sized to fit in the routed grooves in the side and back assemblies. The top panel is made with a ¼-in. × ¼-in. tongue on three sides to fit the top molding. Before you cut stock to length and width, measure the assemblies you've built to make sure you are sizing the parts accurately. The process for making these parts is the same as to make the frame-and-panel parts for the carcase shown in the previous steps, minus the rails.

**1.** Measure the width of the back panel assembly and add ½ in. to determine the length of the bottom and mid-shelf parts. After planing and ripping the parts to width, cut them to length.

**2.** Begin by forming the ½-in. tongues on the front pieces **(PHOTO A)** and on three sides of the panels for the bottom and fixed shelf. These tongues will fit the grooves cut in the sides and back.

**3.** Cut the ¼-in. × ¼-in. tongues on the parts for the top and on one edge of the parts for the fronts of the fixed shelf and bottom. As shown in the drawing on p. 125, the top is composed of three parts, one of which has a ¼-in. × ¼-in. tongue on all four edges, one that has a tongue on both ends and one edge, and a wider panel with a tongue on each end and a groove in both sides **(PHOTO B)**.

**4.** After all the tongues are cut, use the tablesaw to cut the panels to width based on actual measurements. Then cut ¼-in. × ¼-in. grooves on both edges of the top panel and the front edge of the bottom and shelf panels.

**USE A TENONING JIG** to cut the tongues on the bottom and shelf fronts. Size the tongues to fit the grooves in the carcase parts, ¼ in. long × ½ in. thick.

**MAKE THE CUTS ON THE ENDS** first and then the sides. The front and back parts of the top are also shown.

### WORK SMART

I find it helpful to do a trial assembly of the front, back, and one side before cutting the panels to final size. The biscuits in these parts can affect the dimensions of the bottom and shelf. Refer to the sidebar "Sizing Panels" on p. 117.

# Assemble the carcase

**1.** Begin by gluing the front to one side. Put glue in the biscuit slots and just a thin line of glue along the edge of the front and then clamp it in place. Also, put a bit of glue in the front of the middle shelf slot and put the middle shelf front stretcher in place **(PHOTO A)**. You can put the bottom and middle shelves in place as you wait for the glue to set before moving to the next step.

**2.** When the glue holding the front stretcher to one side has set, put biscuits in place to connect the back assembly and clamp it in place **(PHOTO B)**. Check to make sure the subassemblies are square to one another.

**3.** Allow the assembly to rest while the glue sets before adding glue and biscuits to the other side and clamping it in place. Wait at least 45 minutes between steps.

**GLUE AND CLAMP THE FRONT** to one side using #20 biscuits to hold it in position. The middle shelf and bottom can be put in position.

**USE BAR CLAMPS** to hold the back in place. After it has been clamped for 45 minutes or so, continue assembly. Put glue on the edges and biscuits in the slots and clamp the remaining side in place.

# Make the moldings

**THE CROWN AND BASE MOLDINGS ADD** visual interest to the cabinet and give it a finished look. By assembling the crown molding in two sections, additional width and depth is achieved using ¾-in. stock. The crown molding is designed to fit the tongue in the cabinet top. The base molding is fitted in the notch in the front of the cabinet. Attach the base molding with screws driven through the front and sides.

**1.** Begin making the crown molding by planing, jointing, and ripping parts to width. Miter the mating ends to the correct length **(PHOTO A)**.

**TO MAKE THE PARTS FOR THE TOP MOLDINGS,** use a miter gauge set to 45° and cut on the tablesaw.

## Top and crown molding detail

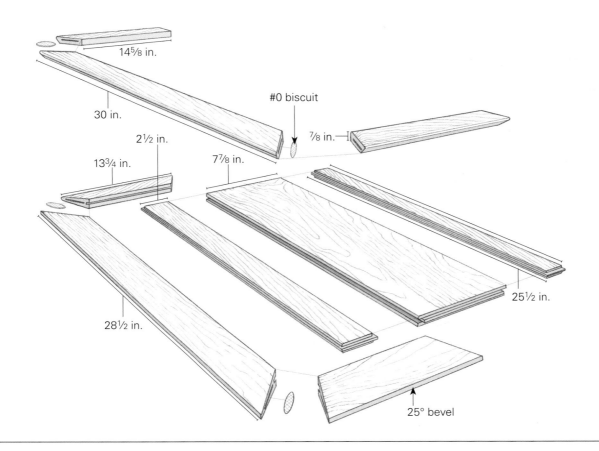

14⅝ in.

30 in.

#0 biscuit

⅞ in.

2½ in.

13¾ in.

7⅞ in.

25½ in.

28½ in.

25° bevel

**B**

CUT GROOVES IN THE INSIDE EDGES of the lower moldings to fit the tongues on the top.

**C**

TILT THE TABLESAW BLADE to cut the molding parts to shape. Use a push block for safety.

**D**

TO ASSEMBLE THE MOLDINGS, use the assembled top unit to help hold the parts in position as the glue sets.

**E**

USE BAR CLAMPS to pull the biscuited joints tight.

**2.** For the three parts that will form the lower section of the crown molding, cut a ¼-in. × ¼-in. groove in the edge to match the tongues cut on the top assembly parts **(PHOTO B)**.

**3.** Then tilt the sawblade 25° to rip one edge from each piece **(PHOTO C)**. You should note that the lower and upper moldings are cut at different angles, so don't do them all at once. In addition to the 42° angle cut on the upper molding parts, I also cut a light 45° chamfer on the upper edges.

**4.** Cut grooves for #0 biscuits on the mitered ends of the molding stock. Practice your biscuit cuts on scrap stock and carefully position the cuts so they're not visible on the outside. Glue and assemble the molding while it is held in position by the top panel assembly **(PHOTO D)**.

**5.** Apply bar clamps to the corners to hold the parts together as the glue sets **(PHOTO E)**.

**6.** To assemble and glue the upper section of the crown molding, cut biscuit slots in the corners, then use tape to hold the parts tight as the glue sets. Clamps won't work for this operation, but by adding layers of tape, a significant amount of clamping pressure can be applied. Pull the tape tight while carefully aligning the parts at the corners. Allow the assembly to lay flat as the glue sets **(PHOTO F)**.

CLAMPS WON'T WORK to hold the upper crown molding while the glue dries, so use packing tape to add pressure after applying glue and inserting the biscuits.

## Make the base molding

**1.** Make the base molding mill stock to $^{11}/_{16}$ in. thick. Rip to a width of $3\frac{1}{2}$ in. and rip a 30° bevel $\frac{1}{4}$ in. from the inside face of the top edge.

**2.** Tilt the tablesaw blade to 45°. Using a miter sled (or miter gauge), cut the parts to length. Note that the miter cuts are made only on the ends of the front piece and at one end of each side piece **(PHOTO G)**. Make the miter cuts on the side pieces first and clamp them in place so that you can take exact measurements. In fitting the front piece of molding, I prefer to cut it slightly long at first then gradually trim it shorter to a perfect fit.

**3.** Sand the parts before installation. If you prefer, you can remove, sand, and replace the parts after they have been fitted to the cabinet. Use C-clamps to hold the parts in place as you drive screws through the side and front assemblies to hold the molding parts in place **(PHOTO H)**.

MITER THE MATING ENDS of the base molding stock and fit the molding to the cabinet.

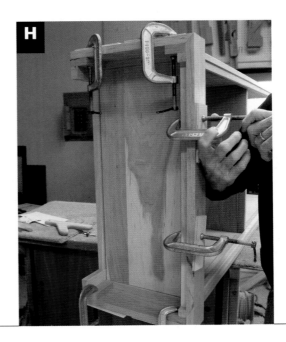

CLAMP THE BASE MOLDING parts in place so you can predrill from the inside for the attachment screws. Use a depth stop to avoid drilling through.

# Assemble and install the top

**THE EASIEST WAY TO ATTACH THE UPPER**
crown molding is the way a trim carpenter might
do it. Lay a small bead of wood glue along the top
of the lower section of crown molding, position the
upper section in place and then use a brad nailer
to secure it. Align the back ends of the upper and
lower sections and then slide the upper section
left or right as necessary so the one is centered over
the other.

**B**

**SECURE THE TOP** with predrilled and countersunk #6 screws. Drive them through the top
into the sides and back.

**A**

**LAY A BEAD OF GLUE** between the bottom and top
molding, then secure the two parts with a brad nailer.

**1.** Lay a bead of glue on the lower crown. Arrange
the top pieces in place. Drive 1³⁄₁₆-in. brads from the
upper section into the lower **(PHOTO A)**.

**2.** To install the cabinet top, leave the top molding in place partially surrounding the top assembly.
Align the back edge of the top assembly with the
back edge of the cabinet and use screws driven from
the top into the sides and back **(PHOTO B)**. Predrill
and countersink the screws so they will be flush. I
use #6 × 1¼-in. long screws. After the back section
of the cabinet top is in place, align the ends of the
top molding with the edge of the back section of the
top. Then align the front part of the top assembly
with the front edges of the cabinet sides; use wood
screws to secure it in place. Center the middle piece
of the top assembly with an equal amount of space
for contraction and expansion on each side, and use
an additional centered screw at each end to secure it
to the cabinet sides.

## TAPE, NOT NAILS

The angled surfaces will make gluing and clamping
difficult. So, before the top assembly is attached to
the cabinet sides and back, use clear packing tape
to hold the parts together and in alignment as the
glue sets. I often use several layers of tape to build
up sufficient clamping pressure. Using clear tape will
allow you to see that the parts are in alignment. Only
a small amount of glue should be used.

# Build the doors

**YOU COULD BUILD THE DOOR FRAMES WITH** biscuits, but bridle joints provide more strength and help keep the frames flat during assembly.

**1.** Begin by carefully selecting your material with an eye to matching the grain in the parts. Mark each piece as it is cut and positioned so you can remember where it will go in the finished doors **(PHOTO A)**.

**2.** Cut the bridle slots in the ends of the door stiles using a tenoning jig. Keep the back side of the stock against the jig and widen the cut in two steps to ¼ in. wide. The blade height is set to $2^{17}/_{32}$ in. ($2½$ in. for the height of the rail tenons plus $1/_{32}$ in. for trimming the doors) **(PHOTO B)**.

**3.** Cut the ¼-in. shoulders for the rail tenons on a crosscut sled. Set the stop block $2^{1}/_{32}$ in. from the outside edge of the blade **(PHOTO C)**.

**4.** Complete the rail tenons by cutting the cheeks with a tenoning jig. Set the blade height at $2^{1}/_{32}$ in. Make test cuts on scrap before cutting your project wood. Keep the back side of the stock against the fence to ensure a uniform fit of all the frame parts **(PHOTO D)**.

**ARRANGE THE STOCK FOR THE FRAME** to achieve the best grain match. Mark the parts carefully so you'll remember where each goes.

**CUT THE BRIDLE SLOTS** with a tenoning jig. Keep the back face of the frame against the jig. Widen the slot to ¼ in. on a second pass.

**CUT THE RAIL TENON SHOULDERS** on the crosscut sled with the stop block positioned $2^{1}/_{32}$ in. from the blade.

**CUT THE RAIL TENON CHEEKS** with the tenoning jig. Set the blade height at $2^{17}/_{32}$ in.

**5.** Trim the rail tenons to their final width of 2½ in. Set a stop block 2½ in. from the blade. The outside edge of the rail is positioned against the stop block. Raise the blade nearly to the height of the shoulder of the tenon when the stock is on end.

**6.** Use a sliding stop block to position the parts for the next cuts. Slide the stop block to the operator's left, to set the position so that the blade cut aligns with the shoulder of the tenon. Slide the stop block out of the way during the cut to prevent trapping of the waste **(PHOTO E)**.

**TRIM THE RAIL TENONS** to the final width of 2½ in. by cutting along the shoulder into the vertical cut. Use a sliding stop block on the sled to control the position of the cut and prevent trapping the offcut.

## Shape and groove the rails

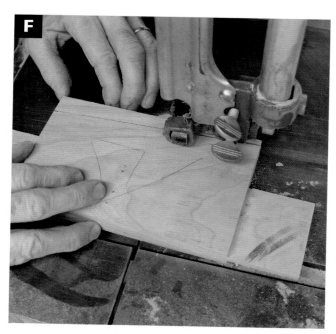

**CUT THE 4° ANGLE** in the top rail on the bandsaw. Then smooth the cut with a handplane or by taking light cuts on the jointer.

I planned the grooves to fit within the bridle slots on the door stiles so they wouldn't show on the outside of the doors. To position the groove, I rely on settings taken from the stiles. To prepare for this operation, I first cut the top rail to its final shape using a bandsaw and jointer. The 4° angle on the top rail is intended to reflect the angular design of the top moldings.

**1.** Make a pencil mark 3¼ in. from the top outside corner along the edge, and one 4 in. down from the other and draw a pencil line between the two. This will give you a 4° angle. Using a bandsaw, cut on the waste side of the pencil line **(PHOTO F)**.

**2.** Smooth the sawn edges of the bandsaw cut with a sharp handplane or by taking light cuts on the jointer.

**3.** Cut the grooves in all the door parts for the raised panels to fit. The tongues on the panels need not be any specific size. My preference is that they fit between the open mortises at the ends of the door stiles so that the grooves cut for them to fit will not be visible on the edges of the doors. This

TO POSITION THE GROOVE in the door frames, carefully adjust the rip fence so that the blade will cut just inside the bridle slot on the stiles.

ADJUST THE FENCE TO WIDEN THE CUT so the blade is inside the opposite bridal leg. Hold the same face of the stock against the fence for each cut.

operation requires two tablesaw setups, both with the blade height at ¼ in. but with the fence in two positions. I use one of the door stiles to guide my setup, by setting the blade to fit inside the bridle slot without rubbing against the stock (PHOTO G). Cut one side of the groove on each part.

**4.** Then set the fence so that the blade will cut just inside the opposite leg of the bridle (PHOTO H). Again, it should be close but not touching. Finish cutting the grooves to width.

## Make the door panels

To make the raised panels for the front of the cabinet, I chose sugar maple to provide color contrast. You could choose a wood to match the rest of the cabinet or choose from any number of interesting woods. Species with a more distinctive grain will work well, or you could make resawn book-matched panels for even greater appeal.

**1.** Plane and rip the panels to width. Square one end of each but leave the top end uncut. Cut the ¼-in. × ¼-in. tongues on three sides. (Adjust the tongue thickness to fit the grooves in the frame.)

**2.** Use a dry-assembled frame as a template to mark off where the panel will meet the frame (PHOTO I). Flip the frame to mark the other panel so the top angle of each is going in the right direction.

MARK OFF THE ANGLE of the top cut using a dry-assembled frame.

**J**

**LAY OUT THE CUT LINE,** using an angle gauge or sliding T-bevel positioned ¼ in. away from the traced line as shown.

**K**

**USE A ³⁄₈-IN.-RADIUS CORE-BOX BIT** to profile the raised panels. Take light cuts and raise the height of the cutter in steps. Rout the short-grain ends first so that you can clean up tearout with the long-grain cuts.

**3.** Use an angle gauge or sliding T-bevel to mark a cut line ¼ in. from the line marked using the door as your guide **(PHOTO J)**.

**4.** Set the miter gauge on the tablesaw to the necessary angle and cut each door panel along the line. This operation can also be done with the bandsaw, or with a hand-held jigsaw or circular saw set up with a guide fence. When the panels have been cut to shape, finish forming the tongues on the top ends.

**5.** Raise the panel with a ³⁄₈-in.-radius core-box bit (see the sidebar below) by raising the bit height in increments **(PHOTO K)**.

**6.** Before assembly, rout into the inside corners of the door stiles and rails as you did on the side and back assemblies and use a straight chisel to finish the cuts at each inside corner (see p. 119.)

**7.** Sand both sides of the raised panels before assembly and also sand the inside edges of the stiles and rails, as these parts can't be sanded afterward.

**8.** Spread glue on the tenons and on the insides of the mortises before you push the parts together. Depending on how tight your tenons fit, some clamping may be required to pull the parts into position. Use C-clamps to compress the bridle legs against the tenons and allow 45 minutes or longer for the glue to set.

**9.** Make the door retainer strip (see the drawing below) and glue it to the inner stile of one door.

## PROFILING THE PANEL

One of the mistakes woodworkers make in small cabinets is to use tools designed for kitchen cabinetry, when the scale of the work really calls for a more delicate approach. For the decorative edge on these panels, I chose a ³⁄₈-in.-radius core-box bit which is designed to form a simple cove cut. By positioning the fence slightly away from the center of the bit, and with the bit raised ⅛ in. to ³⁄₁₆ in. above the surface of the router table, take test cuts on scrap wood until you get the right profile. It helps when working with woods as hard as this maple to take the cut in a series of smaller steps, either raising the bit or moving the fence to work up to a deeper cut.

# Cross-section of door strip

Cut the rabbets on the tablesaw after cutting the 45° chamfer on the outside face on the router table. Make the ¾-in. cuts first, with the back of the strip on edge.

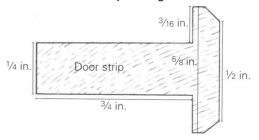

³⁄₁₆ in.

¼ in.  Door strip  ⁵⁄₈ in.

½ in.

¾ in.

# Prepare for the hardware and shelves

**THERE ARE SIX HINGE MORTISES TO CUT, SO** I used a router and template.

**1.** Rout the hinge mortises in the front stiles of the cabinet sides and the outer stiles of the doors **(PHOTO A)**. Begin by laying out the centerlines of the hinge mortises from the top of the doors at 6 in., 27 in., and 48 in. Add ¹⁄₁₆ in. to each location for the carcase hinge mortises to provide clearance for the door. The mortises are ⅝ in. wide. Add two layers of card stock (about ¹⁄₃₂ in.) to shim the template when routing the mortises in the carcase to prevent binding. See pp. 49–51 for how to build and use a hinge template.

**2.** Use a drilling template to position the shelf pins **(PHOTO B)**. I spaced the pin holes ⁷⁄₁₆ in. on center from the inside edge of the side stiles. There are 21 holes above the fixed shelf and 11 holes below, spaced 1 in. on center. The lower holes begin 6 in. up from the bottom, and the upper holes, 6 in. up from the fixed shelf. Drill the holes ½ in. deep, using a piece of dowel as a stop.

**ROUT THE HINGE MORTISES** using a shopmade hinge template. Note the card stock used to shim the position of the template for routing the mortises in the doors.

**3.** Install a magnetic catch underneath the fixed shelf. Position the catch equally between each door **(PHOTO C)**, and add commercial or shop-turned pulls of your choice.

**MAKE A DRILLING TEMPLATE** to position the shelf pin holes. A piece of dowel serves as a stop.

**INSTALL A MAGNETIC CATCH** under the fixed shelf to retain the doors in place when closed.

# Krenov-Inspired Cabinet

**J**AMES KRENOV IS one of the best-known and most influential American cabinetmakers. Reflecting his training in Scandinavia, his designs present a simple elegance. A small cabinet on a stand is one of Krenov's signature designs. My objective in making this piece was not to build a reproduction, but to engage in a thoughtful dialog with his now classic cabinet design.

I built this cabinet from maple. The doors and stand are figured wood, while the sides and top are straight-grained wood, allowing me to cut dovetails more easily. You can use another species, or simplify the project to suit your skill set. For example, you could use biscuits or dowels to connect the top and bottom to the sides instead of the more challenging dovetail joints. While I made this cabinet and base with an angled front and hand-cut dovetailed drawer, you can simplify the project by making the front flat and eliminating the drawer.

# Krenov-inspired cabinet

This cabinet-on-stand project will give you an opportunity to practice and refine your technique for cutting dovetails by hand. Just as I took inspiration from Krenov's work, I hope you'll use this design as a starting point to develop your own interpretation.

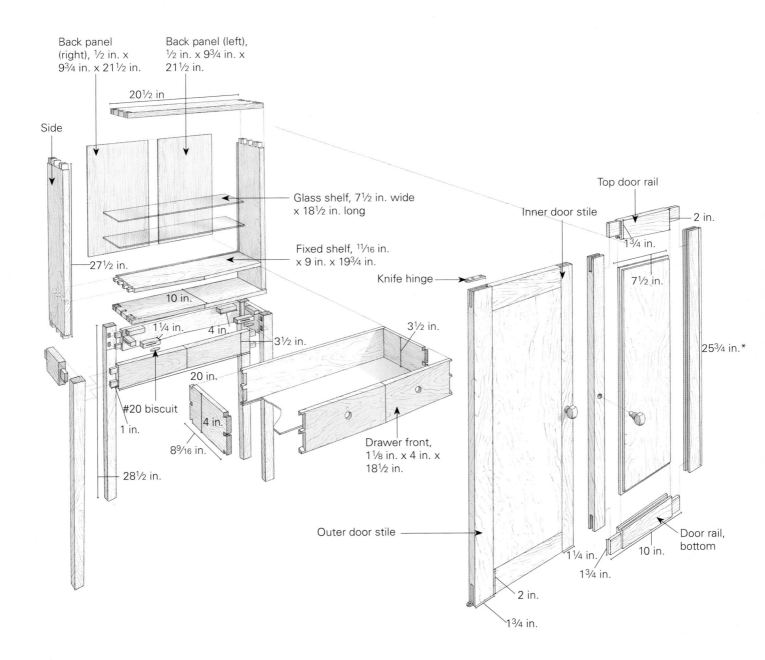

Back panel (right), ½ in. x 9¾ in. x 21½ in.

Back panel (left), ½ in. x 9¾ in. x 21½ in.

20½ in

Side

Glass shelf, 7½ in. wide x 18½ in. long

27½ in.

Fixed shelf, ¹¹⁄₁₆ in. x 9 in. x 19¾ in.

10 in.

1¼ in.

4 in.

3½ in.

3½ in.

20 in.

#20 biscuit

1 in.

4 in.

8⁹⁄₁₆ in.

28½ in.

Drawer front, 1⅛ in. x 4 in. x 18½ in.

Outer door stile

Top door rail

Inner door stile

2 in.

1¾ in.

Knife hinge

7½ in.

25¾ in.*

1¼ in.

10 in.

Door rail, bottom

1¾ in.

2 in.

1¾ in.

*Trim to final length after assembly.

# MATERIALS FOR KRENOV-INSPIRED CABINET

| QUANTITY | PART | SIZE | NOTES |
|---|---|---|---|
| 2 | Top and Bottom | ¾ in. x 10 in. x 20½ in. | Maple |
| 2 | Sides | ¾ in. x 8⁹⁄₁₆ in. x 27½ in.* | Maple |
| 2 | Fixed shelves | ¹¹⁄₁₆ in. x 9 in. x 19¾ in. | Maple |
| 1 | Back panel (left) | ½ in. x 9½ in. x 21½ in. | Maple |
| 1 | Back panel (right) | ½ in. x 9¾ in. x 21½ in. | Maple |
| 2 | Outer door stiles | ¹¹⁄₁₆ in. x 1¾ in. x 25¾ in.† | Maple |
| 2 | Inner door stiles | ¹¹⁄₁₆ in. x 1¼ in. x 25¾ in.† | Maple |
| 4 | Door rails | ¹¹⁄₁₆ in. x 2 in. x 10½ in.† | Maple |
| 2 | Door panels | ¹¹⁄₁₆ in. x 7½ in. x 22¾ in. | Maple |
| 4 | Legs | 1½ in. x 1½ in. x 29½ in. | Maple |
| 1 | Front apron | 1⅜ in. x 3½ in. x 20 in. | Maple |
| 2 | Side aprons | ⅞ in. x 3½ in. x 8¹⁵⁄₁₆ in. | Maple |
| 1 | Rear apron | ⅞ in. x 3½ in. x 20 in. | Maple |
| 6 | Biscuit blocks | ¾ in. x 1¼ in. x 4 in. | Maple |
| 6 | Biscuits | #20 | |
| 1 | Drawer front | 1⅛ in. x 4 in. 18½ in. | Maple |
| 2 | Drawer sides | ⁷⁄₁₆ in. x 4 in. x 8⁹⁄₁₆ in. | Maple |
| 1 | Drawer back | ⁷⁄₁₆ in. x 4 in. x 18½ in. | Maple |
| 1 | Drawer bottom | ¼ in. x 8 in. x 18⅛ in. | Baltic-birch plywood |
| 3 | Stop pins | ³⁄₁₆ in. dia. x ½ in. | Brass stock |
| 2 pr. | Knife hinges | ⅜ in. x 1¾ in. | Brusso®, Woodcraft #145289 |
| 2 | Door pulls | 1⅜ in. x 1⅜ in. x 1⅛ in. | Turn from 1½-in. x ½-in. x 7-in. block of maple |
| 12 | Steel wood screws | #6 x 1¼ in. | |
| 4 | Leg tips | ⅝ in. dia. | 3 prong |
| 2 | Door magnets | | Woodcraft #149508 |
| 2 | Glass shelves | ¼ in. x 7½ in. x 18½ in. | Edges polished |
| 8 | Shelf pins | ¼ in. dia. | Woodcraft #145295 |

*Trim to final dimensions with a 3° angle at the front edge after the dovetail pins are cut. If using dowels or biscuits, the length should be 25¾ in. †Trim excess length after assembly.

# Cut the dovetail joints

**CUTTING DOVETAILS BY HAND REQUIRES** some practice. Before working on the wood you'll use in the project, warm up by practicing on a less expensive species like poplar. In laying out the dovetails, I planned the wide part of the pins to be the same width as my ⅜-in. chisel and laid them out using a sliding T-bevel. Variable spacing between dovetails is a sign that the joint is handcut, but the actual spacing is a matter of personal preference.

**MEASURE AND MARK** the position of the pins. Use a sliding T-bevel to lay them out at the correct angle. I use a fine-tipped black pen for the clearest mark.

**LAY A GAUGE LINE** on the cabinet top, bottom, and sides to define the depth of your pins and tails.

**1.** Use a marking gauge to lay the baselines that will serve as stopping point for the saw and provide a place to rest the chisel to define cut. Set the pin of the marking gauge at 1 in. to mark the top and bottom so that the ¾-in. sides will be inset by ¼ in. **(PHOTO A)**. Set the marking gauge at ⅞ in. for marking the sides so the top and bottom will protrude by ⅛ in.

**2.** Set a sliding bevel at a ratio of 1:8, which is suggested by many craftsmen as ideal for hardwoods. Measure the desired spacing for the pins. Mark the ends of the pins with a fine-tipped pen or sharp pencil and use the sliding bevel as your guide for the correct angle **(PHOTO B)**.

**EXTEND THE MARKS** down to the gauge line on the outside of the stock. Use a small square to guide the pen or sharp pencil.

**3.** Continue the lines down to the marking gauge line on the outside of the stock using a square and fine-tipped pen **(PHOTO C)**.

## WORK SMART

I find it helpful to mark the areas to be removed between the pins. This reminds me which side of the line I should be cutting on.

# Cut the pins

**1.** Cut the pin lines down to the marking gauge lines on both sides of the stock. Use a backsaw—either a Japanese dozuki saw or a traditional dovetail saw (**PHOTO D**).

**D**

**CUT DOWN TO THE GAUGE LINE.** Hold the sawblade level as you finish the cut to make sure it intersects the gauge line on both sides of the stock.

**E**

**REMOVE SOME OF THE WASTE** with a bandsaw. Make sure to perform this operation with the outside face down so you can see where you're cutting and avoid the pins.

**2.** Use a bandsaw to cut away some of the waste from between the pins. This will make chiseling much easier and faster. Make sure that you have the stock with the outside face side down on the bandsaw table so you avoid cutting into the pins (**PHOTO E**). You could also use a coping saw or a scrollsaw to remove the excess waste.

**3.** Remove the remaining waste with a chisel, cutting in from both sides. I remove almost all the waste about 1/16 in. from the marking gauge line and leave the rest in place for a final trimming cut (**PHOTO F**).

**CUT AWAY THE WASTE** between the pins with a sharp chisel. Make your first cuts away from the marking gauge line. Then use the line to provide a clear starting point for final cleanup and removal of the waste between the pins.

**F**

# Cut the tails

**1.** Clamp a guide piece along the marking gauge line to help hold the cabinet parts in place while you mark the locations for the dovetails. Use a piece of stock about 1½ in. sq. so that you can clamp it to the cabinet top or bottom and also clamp from the other direction to hold the cabinet side. Note that the parts align at the back. Once you have positioned the parts, trace the shape of the pins with a knife **(PHOTO G)**.

**2.** Continue the marks to the end of the stock using a knife and square **(PHOTO H)**.

**3.** Cut down to the gauge line with a backsaw (a dozuki saw or dovetail saw) **(PHOTO I)**.

**4.** Use a drill press and ¼-in. bit to drill between the dovetails to begin removing waste between them. This improves both the speed and accuracy with which the joints can be cut. You could also remove this waste with a coping saw.

**USE A SQUARE** to extend the dovetail marks to the end of the stock. Use a knife for marking, as the final cuts must be precise.

**CUT ALONG THE DOVETAIL LINES** using a backsaw. Cut down to the gauge lines on both sides.

**WORK SMART**

A knife gives a much more precise line than a pencil or pen when tracing pins. It will also provide an indentation to provide a place to position the edge of the chisel for the final trimming cuts.

**TRACE THE PINS WITH A KNIFE. Clamp the cabinet side to a board aligned to the gauge line on the mating part while you define the shape of the dovetails.**

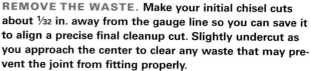

**REMOVE THE WASTE.** Make your initial chisel cuts about 1/32 in. away from the gauge line so you can save it to align a precise final cleanup cut. Slightly undercut as you approach the center to clear any waste that may prevent the joint from fitting properly.

**5.** Chop out the remaining waste with a chisel. As you begin, stay slightly away from the gauge lines so that these will remain for your final cuts **(PHOTO J).** Use the gauge line to place your final trim cuts.

**6.** Angle the chisel very slightly in toward the center to make certain there is a bit of wiggle room as the joint is tested and assembled **(PHOTO K).**

**7.** Fit the joints, noting how the pins and tails come together, so you can anticipate any difficulties before assembly **(PHOTO L).**

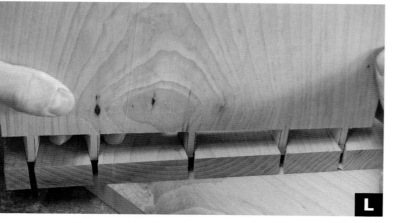

**CHECK THE FIT OF THE JOINT.** Some additional minor chiseling may be required to get a perfect fit.

# Complete the carcase

**CUT THE TENON SHOULDERS.** A stop block positions the stock to be cut at 5/8 in. from the edge. The blade is raised slightly less than 3/16 in. above the sled surface.

**TO ADD VISUAL INTEREST TO THE CABINET,** I've made the front so it angles where the double doors meet at the center. This is accomplished by cutting a 3° angle in the top, bottom, and sides. The carcase has a fixed shelf, providing a division of the space for the drawer.

**1.** Define the tenon shoulders on the edges of the fixed shelf by cutting with the blade raised to slightly less than 3/16 in. above the surface of the sled. Set the stop block to cut 5/8 in. from the edge **(PHOTO A).**

**CUT THE TENON CHEEKS** by standing the stock on edge. Keeping the same surface toward the fence, remove material on each side to make a ⅜-in.-thick tenon.

**2.** Stand the shelf on end to trim the tenons to a ⅜-in. thickness. I make the cuts on both sides, but with the same surface against the fence for both cuts. Move the fence to change the location of the cut **(PHOTO B)**.

**3.** Lay out the tenons. The rear tenon is 1 in. from the edge to accommodate the groove for the back. The front tenon is 9⁄16 in. from the edge. (The front will be trimmed to form a 3° angle later.) The remaining tenons are spaced 1 in. apart. Use the sled and stop block on the tablesaw to define the ends of the tenons and then nibble away with the saw to form the spaces between **(PHOTO C)**.

**4.** Trim the outside tenons to width on the sled with the long-grain side of the shelf on edge.

**5.** Lay out the mortises in the carcase sides to reflect the pattern of the tenons you just cut. Remember that the wider space between the edge and the end tenon goes toward the back to accommodate the groove for the back. The bottom of the fixed shelf is 4⅞ in. from the bottom of the sides, which puts the tenons at 5¹⁄16 in. from the bottom of the sides. Use a plunge router and a guide fence clamped in place to rout the mortises **(PHOTO D)**. To locate the guide fence, you will need to measure the distance from the edge of the cut to the edge of the router base and add that measurement to the distance from the end of the stock to the planned location of the tenons. Mark the start and stop positions

**FINISH FORMING THE TENONS** by using a tablesaw sled and stop blocks to position the cuts. Nibble away the waste between the tenons ⅛ in. at a time.

**ROUT THE MORTISES.** Clamp a piece of stock to the side to use as a guide for the plunge router. I use a ⅜-in. upcut spiral router bit for the smoothest cut.

for the plunge router. I rout the mortises slightly longer than is actually required so that I can avoid having to chisel the corners square. The mortises should be routed to a depth of ⅝ in. so they don't go all the way through the stock.

# Cut the angles

**1.** Cut the top and bottom using a precision miter gauge on the tablesaw with a stop block clamped in place to control the position of the cut. To set up the stop block, find the point where the blade hits a centerline marked at the front of the part. Turn the stock over end for end to cut the opposite side **(PHOTO E)**.

**2.** Tilt the blade of the saw to a 3° angle and set the rip fence to trim the cabinet sides to correspond with the angles in the top and bottom.

**E**

**CUT THE 3° ANGLE** on the top, bottom, and shelf from the front center to each end. I use a precision miter gauge and stop block to position each cut.

# Make the back

**CUT TONGUES** on the outside edges off the back panel on the table-saw. Cut a tongue-and-groove joint at the intersection of the two panels.

**F**

**G**

**ROUT THE GROOVE FOR THE BACK.** Set the router fence so that the cut is ⁹⁄₁₆ in. from the edge of the stock.

**1.** Begin by planing stock to a thickness of ⅝ in. Glue pieces together to form panels approximately 10 in. wide to make the two halves of the back. Then plane the stock to a thickness of ½ in. Cut the two-piece back panel to length and final width on the tablesaw. (Note that the two panels are different widths because of the tongue-and-groove joint.)

**2.** Cut ¼-in. × ¼-in. tongues on the outside edges of the panels where they will fit into the cabinet sides, top, and center shelf **(PHOTO F)**. Cut a tongue-and-groove joint to form the connection between the two (see pp. 102–103 for more information on cutting tongues and tongue-and-groove assemblies).

**3.** Rout ¼-in.-wide grooves to a depth of ¼ in. for the back panel in the cabinet sides, top, and the top of the fixed shelf. Use a plunge router and a ¼-in. upcut spiral router bit. Set the fence so the router bit cuts ⁹⁄₁₆ in. from the back edge of the parts **(PHOTO G)**.

# Prepare for assembly

**1.** Drill the shelf support holes 1½ in. from the front and back edges of the cabinet sides. The ¼-in. holes are ½ in. deep, spaced 1 in. apart. There are 12 holes, beginning 5 in. up from the fixed shelf (10½ in. up from the bottom of the cabinet side). I laid out the pencil lines and used a guide fence on the drill press to hold the stock at the correct distance for drilling **(PHOTO H)**.

**2.** Rout the mortises for the knife hinges. Mark start and stop positions for travel of the plunge router and set the router depth to correspond with the thickness of the hinge leaf so it will come out flush on the surface and not interfere with the movement of the drawer **(PHOTO I)**. For more information on laying out and routing mortises for knife hinges, see pp. 65–66 and 71–73.

**3.** Rout the underside of the fixed shelf for a stop to prevent the door from coming all the way out. Use a ¾-in. router bit in the plunge router and cut ¼ in. deep. Cut from the back edge to a distance 1¼ in. from the front edge **(PHOTO J)**.

**DRILL ¼-IN. HOLES FOR THE SHELF SUPPORTS.** Clamp a fence to the table to align the holes a uniform distance of 1½ in. from the edges of the stock.

**4.** Sand all the parts thoroughly before assembly. I use a series of grits from 150 through 320. To soften all the edges I use a chamfering bit in the router for some parts and use a plane for others, as shown in **PHOTO M** on p. 151. As an alternative, a sanding block can be used. Shape the end grain first and then work on the side grain. Also sand the pins on the sides to a slight chamfer. This not only will make them look better in the finished cabinet, but also will ease their path during assembly.

**ROUT THE MORTISES FOR THE KNIFE HINGES.** Use a ⅜-in. straight router bit. The fence keeps the bit the precise distance from the edge and penciled points indicate stopping and starting locations for the router.

**ROUT THE FIXED SHELF** with a ¾-in. router bit to a depth of ⁵⁄₁₆ in. This groove will be for the drawer stop.

WORK
**SMART**

When drilling shelf-pin holes, a brad-point bit helps align the stock for more accurate drilling.

**APPLY GLUE TO THE PINS. Be careful to avoid getting glue on the portions of the joint that will be exposed on the outside of the cabinet.**

**1.** Do a trial assembly to avoid difficulties fitting the parts after gluing. If the parts have to be forced, either the top or side could split so it's better to make adjustments rather than force too hard. When you're satisfied with the fit, apply glue to the inside of the mortise and put the fixed shelf in place, joining the two sides. Insert the back panel in the grooves. Carefully apply glue to the pins **(PHOTO K)**. Apply the glue only where it will not be seen in the assembled joint. Then put the top panel in place.

**2.** Light tapping with a small mallet should drive the joint home. Use a block of wood to cushion the force and prevent marring the surface below. When the top is in place, turn the carcase over and install the bottom.

# Build the base

**THE MORTISES ARE ARRANGED TO BYPASS** at the corners rather than intersecting and weakening the joint, so lay out the joinery carefully.

**1.** Mill the parts for the cabinet base from solid maple stock. Begin by milling the legs to 1½ in. × 1½ in. and cutting them to length.

**2.** Carefully lay out the leg mortises (see the drawing on the facing page). Before layout, decide on the most pleasing arrangement of the grain and use a system to keep track of the outside surfaces of adjacent legs so that you'll know where the leg belongs in the finished base. Lay out the mortises with a ruler and square **(PHOTO A)**. Note that the front and rear aprons each have two tenons on each end, so the corresponding leg surfaces have two mortises. The side aprons have one larger tenon on each end.

**LAY OUT THE LEG MORTISES** with a ruler, pencil, and square. Mark each leg to keep track of its position in the base. Mortises are ⅜ in. wide and ⅜ in. from the outside edge of the leg.

**B**

**CUT THE MORTISES** slightly over 1 in. deep using a hollow chisel mortiser with a ³⁄₈-in.-square chisel. Set the fence so the mortises are ³⁄₈ in. from the outside surfaces of the legs.

**3.** Set a stop block and the fence to control the position of the stock relative to the chisel. Cut to a depth slightly over 1 in. This ensures that the 1-in.-long tenons will seat properly during assembly **(PHOTO B)**.

**4.** Tilt the tablesaw blade to 3° and make a ripping cut along the front side of each front leg with the mortised side up. This will give the front legs the same angle as the carcase **(PHOTO C)**.

**5.** Taper the legs on the inside surfaces only from a point 4 in. down from the top. This will result in the base of the leg being 1 in. sq. The distance of 4 in. from the top will keep the taper from interfering with the mortise-and-tenon joints connecting the aprons to the legs. To lay out the taper, draw a line 4 in. from the top to a mark inset ½ in. on the inside surfaces of the leg. Cut the taper on the bandsaw **(PHOTO D)**.

Since the front legs have been shaped to match the front, no cut should be made on those using the front surface down. Clean up the saw marks on the jointer or use a sharp handplane. A very precise bandsawn line will keep your cleanup to a minimum and keep the shape intact.

## Leg layout detail

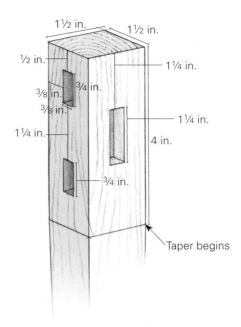

**C**

**RIP A 3° ANGLE** on the front face of the front legs.

**D**

**CUT A TAPER** on the insides of the legs on the bandsaw. The taper begins 4 in. down from the top of the leg.

# Make the aprons and assemble the base

**CUT THE TENON SHOULDERS** on a crosscut sled. Set a stop block to establish a tenon length of 1 in.

**REMOVE THE WASTE** between the double tenons by taking repetitive passes over the blade. Each cut removes ⅛ in.

**CUT THE TENONS** to a thickness of ⅜ in. Use a tenoning jig. Remember to keep the same surface against the jig for consistently placed tenons.

**1.** Mill the stock for the aprons. The stock for the back and side aprons should measure ⅞ in. thick. The front apron is 1⅜ in. thick to allow it to be shaped to the same angles as the carcase. Cut the stock to width and length.

**2.** Cut the shoulders for the tenons on the tablesaw sled with a stop block set to make a cut 1 in. from the edge of each apron. For all but the front side of the front apron, set the blade height at ¼ in. above the sled table **(PHOTO E)**. For the front side of the thicker front apron, set the blade height at ¾ in. Cut from both sides so that the tenon will be ⅜ in. thick.

**3.** Cut the tenons to width. Place the apron on end. Use a sled and stop block to define the cut. Then make a series of repetitive cuts to remove the waste between the double tenons on the front and rear aprons **(PHOTO F)**.

**4.** Cut the tenons to ⅜ in. thick, using a tablesaw tenoning jig. In adjusting the tenon thickness, use mortises cut in the legs for a test fit. Cutting a test tenon on scrap stock can help you fine-tune the fit **(PHOTO G)**.

**CUT THE FRONT** and back aprons to shape using the bandaw.

**CUT THE ANGLES** in the front stretcher on the bandsaw. Then smooth the cut by scraping and sanding.

**5.** Mark each end ½ in. in from the front face with the stock on edge. Connect these marks to the center point of the front face. Cut the angles on the bandsaw **(PHOTO H)**.

**6.** Mark out the angle at the bottom of the front and back aprons. The stock should be back face down. Measure in ¾ in. from the center of the bottom and draw a line from this point to the bottom end of each side of the stretch. Cut away the waste on the bandsaw **(PHOTO I)**.

**7.** Cut biscuit slots on the inside of each apron to hold the biscuit blocks. These blocks will secure the carcase to the base. Cut the biscuits about ⅜ in. down from the top inside edge. Center the slot on the short aprons. Cut two slots in the long aprons at approximately 3¼ in. from the end of the apron to the center of the biscuit slot.

**8.** Sand all the parts thoroughly. Chamfer the edges lightly with a router. Then apply glue in each mortise and use bar clamps to pull the joints tight.

# Build the doors

**TO BEGIN MAKING THE CABINET DOORS,** I plane, joint, and rip the frame stock to size and then cut it to length using a sled and stop block so that the paired parts are of equal length. All of the joinery is indexed off the edges of the stock, so it's important that all parts be of consistent width, length, and thickness. You may wish to review the door joinery techniques shown on pp. 42–48.

**1.** Carefully lay out all the door parts and mark them so that the grain in each piece is used to best advantage **(PHOTO A)**. Use a system so that you will know the position of the parts in the final assembly.

**LAY OUT AND MARK** the location for each part. Mark the face sides so you will be able to keep track of which side needs to be against the tenoning jig.

B

CUT THE ¼-IN.-WIDE BRIDLES on the door stiles using a tenoning jig. Keep the front face against the jig for all cuts.

C

CUT THE TENON SHOULDERS 1¾ in. from the edge of the stock. Set a stop block to position the stock.

**2.** Use a tenoning jig to cut the bridle joint slots at the end of each door stile (**PHOTO B**). The front face of the stock is always against the jig. Adjust the cutting distance so that the front leg of the bridle is ³⁄₁₆ in. thick. Make this cut on the ends of all the stiles before adjusting the blade to widen the bridle opening to ¼ in. This leaves the rear leg of the bridle at ¼ in. thick.

**3.** Cut the shoulders of the tenons for each door rail using the sled and stop block to position the cut 1¾ in. from the edge of the rail (**PHOTO C**). Raise the blade to make a ³⁄₁₆-in.-deep cut on the front faces of the rails. Then flip the pieces over to make the ¼-in.-deep cut on the back faces.

**4.** Use a tenoning jig to cut to the shoulder line (**PHOTO D**). The tenons are a nominal ¼ in. thick, but you should fit them to the bridles you cut.

**5.** Use the crosscut sled to trim the inside edge of the tenons. Stand the stock on end and set a stop block to cut the tenons to a width of 1³⁄₁₆ in.

**6.** Cut the last shoulder using a sliding stop block to prevent trapping of the waste between the blade and stop block (**PHOTO E**). Raise the blade to the kerf you cut when the stock was on end.

D

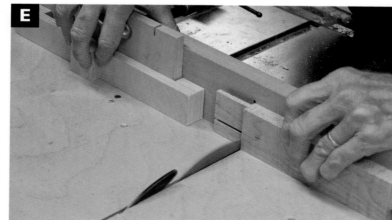

E

TRIM THE TENONS TO FINAL THICKNESS and width to fit the bridles. The tenons and bridle legs will be slightly longer than necessary to allow trimming flush after final assembly.

**F**

LAY OUT A 2° ANGLE ON THE INSIDE EDGES of the door rails. Mark off a point ¼ in. down from the inside edge of the rail and draw a line to the corner.

**7.** Shape the door rails. This must be done after the joints are formed. I planned the door rails to be narrow at the center of the cabinet, adding to the angular look of things. This requires tapering the inside edge of each door rail by a 2° angle, as shown in **PHOTO F**. Mark off ¼ in. from the bottom of the inside edges of each rail and draw a line from this point to the bottom of the outside edge. Make bandsaw cuts along the marked lines, then smooth each cut using the jointer. Your accuracy in making the bandsaw cuts will pay off in less cleanup needed on the jointer.

**8.** Cut a ¼-in.-wide × ¼-in.-deep groove on the inside of the rails and stiles on the tablesaw. Each cut should be made with the back side of the stock against the fence. Adjust the fence location to widen the cut to ¼ in. **(PHOTO G)**.

**G**

CUT ¼-IN. GROOVES for the door panel on the inside edge of the frame members. Keep the rear face of the parts against the fence.

# Make the door panels

**1.** Cut the door panels to width and mark lines indicating the length of the panel before trimming to shape. Draw a pencil line ¼ in. from the bottom end to indicate where the panel will intersect the inside of the frame. Set the dry-assembled door frame in place on top of a door panel and mark one end with a sharp pencil **(PHOTO H)**.

**2.** Move the door frame up along the panel ½ in. to allow for the ¼-in. tongues at each end. Keep the same relationship to the side lines. Then mark the top edge of the panel.

**I**

**CUT THE ANGLE AT EACH END** of the panel using a precision miter gauge aligned to the correct angle.

**H**

**TRACE THE ANGLES.** Place a dry-assembled door over the panel. Trace the shape at each end to indicate where to cut to final length.

**3.** Use a precision miter gauge on the tablesaw to cut along the marked lines to form the shape of the raised panels **(PHOTO I)**.

**4.** Use the tablesaw to form the tongues on the raised panels **(PHOTOS J, K)**. The process for cutting the tongues is very similar to that used in the spice cabinet project; see pp. 45–47 for more detailed information.

**J**

**DEFINE THE THICKNESS OF THE TONGUES** by taking ¼-in. cuts on both faces of the stock, ¼ in. from the edge. Begin with the end grain and then cut the long grain, as shown.

**K**

**COMPLETE THE TONGUES** by cutting with the stock on edge. Again, cut the short-grain sides first so that the long-grain cut can clean up any tearout.

# Complete the doors

**1.** Hold the door frame together using clamps or bench dogs and use a 45° bit to rout a light ⅛-in. chamfer on the inside edges of the door frame. Finish the cut with a straight chisel (**PHOTO L**). First cut directly into the corner with the chisel at a 45° angle and then follow the flat planes provided by the chamfers to finish the cut.

**2.** Use a plane to chamfer the edges of the raised panel. Chamfer the ends first so that any tearout will be removed when the sides are chamfered (**PHOTO M**).

**3.** After all the door parts are assembled, spread glue on the tenons and push the parts tightly together. Check the assembly for square by measuring corner to corner. Adjust as necessary by applying clamp pressure along the long corners. Then use C-clamps with cushion blocks to distribute the clamping pressure to the bridle joints.

**4.** After the doors are assembled, trim the excess tenon length, rout a slight chamfer on the door edges, and cut a slight 3° angle on the inside edges where the doors meet. This will help close the gap.

**5.** Cut the mortises for the knife hinges. First, set the height of the ⅜-in.-dia. straight bit to equal the thickness of one leaf of the knife hinge. Then measure the distance between the cabinet sides and the mortises cut in the base and top. Set the fence with that distance between it and the inside edge of the router cut. Bring the fence forward ¹⁄₃₂ in., clamp it in position, and make a test cut in scrap stock. The test piece will allow you to check the actual clearance between the door and the cabinet carcase. Adjust the fence to get a final clearance of ¹⁄₃₂ in. or greater. Then set up a stop block to control the length of the cut. Hold the corner of the door tightly to the fence and slide it into the stop block to rout the mortise as shown in **PHOTO N**. Use a ⅜-in. chisel to square the cut.

**USE A STRAIGHT** chisel to cut the miters in the corners of the doors.

**CHAMFER THE EDGES OF THE RAISED PANEL.** Plane the end grain first and then the grain along the sides of each panel.

**CUT THE HINGE MORTISES** with a ⅜-in.-dia. router bit. The stop block is carefully placed to control the length of the cut.

# Make the drawer

**CUTTING THE DOVETAILS FOR THE DRAWER** is easy because few are required. Cut the angled drawer front first. Then lay out the joints using a marking gauge, sliding T-bevel, square, pencil, and knife and follow the same steps as required to cut the pins and tails for the carcase.

**CUT THE PINS.** After laying out the pins, cut down to the gauge line using a backsaw.

**1.** Lay out the pins as shown on p. 137, except this time lay out only three pins. On the drawer front, the two pins at the ends are half pins. Lay down a gauge line at $9/16$ in. For the back, you can variably space the pins. Position the gauge line at $1/2$ in.

**2.** Cut the pins down to the gauge line using a backsaw **(PHOTO A)**.

**3.** Remove the waste using a bandsaw or coping saw, followed by cleanup with a sharp chisel **(PHOTO B)**.

**4.** Transfer the layout of the pins to the sides. Lay out the dovetails. Saw to the gauge line and remove the waste.

**REMOVE THE WASTE BETWEEN THE PINS.** Saw away as much of the waste as possible. Then chisel to the gauge line.

**5.** Rout a $1/4$-in.-wide × $1/4$-in.-deep stopped groove on the inside of the parts to hold the bottom. Position the groove $1/4$ in. up from the bottom of the front, sides, and back. Stop the groove just as it enters the dovetailed area. Don't rout through to the edge or it will show on the outside of the drawer **(PHOTO C)**.

**6.** To avoid having drawer pulls that would interfere with closing of the doors, I used finger holes. Use the drill press to drill two 1-in.-dia. finger holes through the front. I located these on center $1^{5}/8$ in. down from the top of the drawer front, and $4^{1}/4$ in. from the center of the drawer.

**ROUT THE STOPPED GROOVES** for the drawer bottom. Mark start and stop lines and rout between.

**7.** Glue and assemble the drawer. To provide positive stops for the drawer to keep it aligned with the back of the cabinet when it is closed, I used a brass pin as a stop. Rout a $^5/_{16}$-in.-wide stopped groove about $1^3/_{16}$ up from the bottom of the drawer sides on the outside for the stop pin. The groove should be about 1 in. long. Once you have the grooves routed, use them to locate where to drill a $^3/_{16}$-in.-dia. hole in each side of the carcase **(PHOTO D)**. Also drill a hole at the center of the top edge of the drawer back for a brass pin to serve as a stop.

**D**

**LOCATE THE DRAWER STOP HOLE** using the groove routed in the assembled drawer. To find the exact spot, align the drawer to the bottom of the carcase side. Position from the back edge of the drawer at a distance equal to the length of the routed groove, about 1 in.

# Final details

**KRENOV'S CABINETS ARE KNOWN FOR** interesting details—hand-carved knobs and pulls, shelf supports, and closure mechanisms. Krenov's cabinetry shares an essential simplicity with other uniquely American woodworking craftsmen, the Shakers. I chose, in dialog between the two, to make my cabinet pulls from a Shaker base.

**1.** Turn Shaker-style knobs on the lathe as shown in making the Shaker cabinet (see p. 21). Trim them to a new shape using the tablesaw. Forming a tight-fitting tenon and two matching knobs is essential to this approach. Use a piece of stock as a sled to carry the knob through the cut. Saw a kerf in the sled to enable you to secure the knob with a screw through the end of the tenon. I tilted the sawblade slightly to enhance the effect **(PHOTO A)**.

**2.** Make the biscuit blocks. Cut the slots while the stock is in one piece. Drill and countersink two screw holes through each **(PHOTO B)**. Then insert biscuits and attach the blocks to the inside of the base. Drive screws through the blocks into the carcase bottom.

**3.** After applying the finish of your choice, install the hinges. Then install the door magnets and pulls.

**A**

**TRIM THE END OF THE SHAKER KNOB** on the tablesaw using a shopmade sled to carry it safely past the blade.

**B**

**DRILL THROUGH THE BISCUIT BLOCKS** on the drill press using stop blocks to control the positions of the holes. Use a countersink so the screws mount flush with the surface of the block.

# Metric Equivalents

| Inches | Centimeters | Millimeters | Inches | Centimeters | Millimeters |
|---|---|---|---|---|---|
| 1/8 | 0.3 | 3 | 13 | 33.0 | 330 |
| 1/4 | 0.6 | 6 | 14 | 35.6 | 356 |
| 3/8 | 1.0 | 10 | 15 | 38.1 | 381 |
| 1/2 | 1.3 | 13 | 16 | 40.6 | 406 |
| 5/8 | 1.6 | 16 | 17 | 43.2 | 432 |
| 3/4 | 1.9 | 19 | 18 | 45.7 | 457 |
| 7/8 | 2.2 | 22 | 19 | 48.3 | 483 |
| 1 | 2.5 | 25 | 20 | 50.8 | 508 |
| 1 1/4 | 3.2 | 32 | 21 | 53.3 | 533 |
| 1 1/2 | 3.8 | 38 | 22 | 55.9 | 559 |
| 1 3/4 | 4.4 | 44 | 23 | 58.4 | 584 |
| 2 | 5.1 | 51 | 24 | 61.0 | 610 |
| 2 1/2 | 6.4 | 64 | 25 | 63.5 | 635 |
| 3 | 7.6 | 76 | 26 | 66.0 | 660 |
| 3 1/2 | 8.9 | 89 | 27 | 68.6 | 686 |
| 4 | 10.2 | 102 | 28 | 71.1 | 711 |
| 4 1/2 | 11.4 | 114 | 29 | 73.7 | 737 |
| 5 | 12.7 | 127 | 30 | 76.2 | 762 |
| 6 | 15.2 | 152 | 31 | 78.7 | 787 |
| 7 | 17.8 | 178 | 32 | 81.3 | 813 |
| 8 | 20.3 | 203 | 33 | 83.8 | 838 |
| 9 | 22.9 | 229 | 34 | 86.4 | 864 |
| 10 | 25.4 | 254 | 35 | 88.9 | 889 |
| 11 | 27.9 | 279 | 36 | 91.4 | 914 |
| 12 | 30.5 | 305 | | | |